PRESENTED TO

_____

FROM

_____

DATE

_____

Millionaire
Answers

SOUND WISDOM BOOKS
BY JIM STOVALL

The Ultimate Gift

The Ultimate Life

The Ultimate Journey

The Ultimate Legacy

The Ultimate Financial Plan

Ultimate Hindsight

Ultimate Productivity

The Millionaire Map

Millionaire Answers

The Gift of a Legacy

A Christmas Snow

Today's the Day!

The Art of Productivity

The Art of Presentation

The Art of Communication

The Art of Entrepreneurship

Millionaire
Answers

25 Years of
Winners' Wisdom
for Building,
Managing, and
Enjoying Wealth

JIM STOVALL

Published and distributed by:
SOUND WISDOM
P.O. Box 310
Shippensburg, PA 17257-0310

717-530-2122

info@soundwisdom.com

www.soundwisdom.com

ISBN 13 TP: 978-1-64095-565-3

ISBN 13 eBook: 978-1-64095-566-0

For Worldwide Distribution, Printed in the U.S.A.

1 2 3 4 5 6 7 8 / 29 28 27 26 25

Dedication

This book is dedicated to my wife, Crystal, who traveled every step of the millionaire journey with me. She gave me the greatest gift anyone could give because she believed in me.

This book is also dedicated to Beth Sharp who took my words and got them onto the page or computer screen you are reading now. As a blind person myself, I don't take this for granted.

And finally, this book is dedicated to the millionaire mentors who have helped me every step of the way. They know who they are, and the only way I can repay them is to help others traveling the same road.

Contents

1

Setting the Stage

I f you are reading this book, I assume you either want to be a millionaire or are exploring the possibility of becoming a millionaire. There are as many reasons for wanting to be a millionaire as there are people pursuing the goal. The only legitimate reason to become a millionaire is that you want to be, do, or have something in your life that requires a million dollars or more. Money is never an end in itself. Instead, money is a tool or vehicle that can get you where you want to go.

I look at it like an electrical extension cord. You have a power outlet across the room and a lamp sitting next to you that will light up everything around you. The cord does not provide electricity, nor does it offer light, but it makes everything possible. If your cord is a fraction of an inch too short or a mile too short, you will be sitting in the dark. On the other hand, if all you want is light for the space around you, having a large quantity of excess cord coiled up on the floor at your feet doesn't make a lot of sense. Wanting to become a millionaire without a corresponding goal is like having an extension cord for no reason.

I clearly remember a time in my early adult life when, as a blind person, I was broke, scared, and drowning in debt with little or no expectation of improving my lot in life. Then I learned some of the principles that you will learn in this book, and my world changed. You have likely not met many people as poor as I was, nor have you encountered too many who enjoy more wealth than I do today.

If you took all the money in the world and divided it up evenly, I believe within a relatively short time, millionaires would reestablish their wealth and poor people would sink back into poverty. Remaining wealthy and living with wealth is actually more difficult than becoming a millionaire in the first place. Millionaires turn their knowledge into habits that continue to multiply their wealth. Poor people continue to suffer in ignorance. Please understand, I am not saying that people in poverty are less intelligent. They simply don't know the steps it takes to become a millionaire.

For over a quarter of a century, I have written a syndicated column entitled *Winners' Wisdom* that appears in newspapers, magazines, and in online publications around the world. At the end of more than a thousand columns and in each of my more than 50 books, I offer my contact information, and I respond to everyone.

Over the past 25 years, I have received a myriad of questions from countless people. Far and away, the most prevalent topic is that of money, creating wealth, or becoming a millionaire. Throughout this book, you and I will revisit the columns I have written to answer the questions from those who are aspiring to be millionaires.

Whether you are trying to bake a cake, repair a car, or become a millionaire, there are certain ingredients, tools, and techniques that must be utilized. If you bake a cake but leave out one critical ingredient, you will likely have an inedible mess. If 99 percent of the parts in your car engine are intact and working properly, you likely won't be going anywhere. If there are holes or gaps in your millionaire strategy or wealth-building plan, you may be doomed to financial mediocrity.

> Money is not the key to wealth. Knowledge is the key to wealth. Millionaires succeed because they do millionaire things based on millionaire knowledge.

As much as I would like to tell you that every millionaire question will be answered for every reader within these pages, that is quite simply not the case. Everyone's situation is different, and it's impossible to be specific when addressing the multitude. For that reason, I want to encourage you to reach out to me at jim@jimstovall.com with your specific questions or situation. I will endeavor to answer all your questions or refer you to resources where you can get the knowledge you need to live out your financial goals and dreams.

There is probably no topic that attracts more fakes, frauds, and shysters than that of creating wealth and becoming a millionaire.

Approximately a dozen years ago, I wrote a book entitled *The Millionaire Map,* which recounted my own journey from poverty to prosperity. As a blind person, I dictate all of my books, syndicated columns, and screenplays to very talented colleagues who capture my words and get them out to you. As I was dictating *The Millionaire Map,* I heard myself say, "Don't ever take advice from anyone who doesn't have what you want."

I believe everyone's personal business is personal, and it's their own private business right up to the point where they are trying to take some of my time or money based on what they are telling me. Where you may have gone to college and how well you did in your education is totally your business, unless you want me to hire you. Then, your business becomes my business.

After I wrote that section of *The Millionaire Map,* I went home and told my wife, Crystal, that I felt like we were going to have to do something very uncomfortable because my own financial status is your business if you're going to read my books, watch the movies based on them, listen to my speeches, or follow my weekly columns.

As I was writing *The Millionaire Map,* I reached out to Merrill Lynch and Bank of America and asked them to produce a statement on their letterhead that I could publish in my book. This statement confirms that we have no debt, and we have in excess of $10 million in our investment portfolio, which excludes the value of my company, the copyrights on my more than 50 books, as well as the nine movies based on those titles, and all other personal property. Since then, the portfolio has grown significantly even after several $1 million philanthropic gifts through our foundation.

I want you to understand that not only is becoming a millionaire possible, it is the inevitable outcome of applying the principles you will encounter in this book. If I can do this, anyone can do it. There was a time in your life when riding a bicycle, reading printed words on a page, or driving a car seemed impossible until you did it, and now it seems natural and normal.

I'm looking forward to a time in your life when building and maintaining wealth while living a millionaire lifestyle becomes normal and natural.

2

Common Millionaires

J ust as it is impossible to determine someone's religious beliefs, political affiliation, or ancestry simply by meeting them, millionaires often fly under the radar. Success in life is a matter of following the leaders. If you want to be a millionaire, you have to know who they are. The following *Winners' Wisdom* column was written two decades ago to address many questions I have received about who millionaires are and where they can be found. What I wrote then is more true today as we have an exploding number of retirement plan millionaires.

Many of us grew up with images of millionaires as rare and unusual people. Movies and television depicted millionaires as untouchable and unapproachable individuals that common folk could never meet. Here in the 21st century, economic conditions along with the availability of pre-tax investing for everyone have created an environment where millionaires are commonplace. If you stand on a street corner and inquire of everyone who passes by if they are a millionaire or a schoolteacher, you will find that you are three times more likely to meet a millionaire than a schoolteacher.

Today in the United States, there are over 10 million millionaires. While a million dollars won't buy the lifestyle it would have bought for our grandparents, it's certainly better to have a million dollars than to not have a million dollars. Becoming a millionaire is no longer a matter of winning the gene-pool lottery and inheriting your money, or writing a bestseller, signing an NBA contract, or developing a cure for cancer. Becoming a millionaire today is within the reach of almost everyone, but this certainly doesn't mean that the millionaire lifestyle will be lived by everyone.

When I began my working career, I started as an investment broker for a New York Stock Exchange firm. My clients quickly educated me to a reality I had not known before. Looking and acting like a millionaire doesn't make you a millionaire. I had clients who came to my office in brand-new luxury automobiles who lived at the best addresses in town but had low account balances and were constantly borrowing money against their investments to cover expenses. On the other hand, I had clients driving

> Just as common sense will never be common, wealth will never be average. It's a journey available to everyone but remains the road less traveled.

10-year-old cars who lived in very nice but moderate housing and dressed casually who were multimillionaires with a net worth their friends and neighbors would never have imagined.

Trying to look and act like a millionaire before you are one is financially devastating. Farmers who grow corn harvest their crops each year, and those kernels of corn represent not only the product they produce and sell but the seeds they will plant next year. Prevailing wisdom among farmers and wise investors would implore us to "never eat your seed corn." Particularly as a young person, spending beyond one's means instead of investing creates financial disaster. That expensive pair of shoes, oversized car payment, or bit of bling that could otherwise have been an investment would have generated a fortune in the market throughout an investing life.

Financial success is a matter of thinking more of your own financial future than how much you care about what others may think of your current financial condition. Just as common sense will never be common, wealth will never be average. It's a journey available to everyone but remains the road less traveled.

As you go through your day today, make uncommon decisions now so you can live an uncommon life later.

Today's the day!

3

Net Worth
Versus Net Value

I receive many inquiries from people wanting to know how to become a millionaire, but they have never considered why they should become a millionaire. Acquiring wrinkled, dirty pieces of paper with pictures of dead presidents without considering the endgame is mindless folly. It is what I call the Disease of More. Money will never make us better; it will simply make us more than we are. If you're a giving, loving, and caring individual, money will enable you to impact more people positively. On the other hand, if you are greedy, vindictive, and destructive, wealth will make it possible for you to hurt more people.

> Money will never make us better; it will simply make us more than we are.

In the aftermath of my novel, *The Ultimate Gift* and the movie trilogy based on that series, I have had the privilege of consulting with many multimillionaire and billionaire families. I always remind them that transferring your valuables to your children without transferring your values is child abuse. The following column was written in response to questions about who we are as opposed to what we have.

———◆———

Most people in our society have extremely vague or general financial goals. These goals, in some capacity, surround the word "more." These people want more money, more savings, more income, more investments, more retirement, and more stuff. We have become a consumer society. We are bombarded moment to moment by advertisements, commercials, and countless messages telling us that, "You are your stuff." The implication is if you had more, you would be more.

Most people are, at some level, unhappy. The consumer messages tell us that the people who have more than we do are happy. Therefore, we simply need to get more things in our lives. As someone who has been relatively poor and now relatively rich in my life, I can echo the old adage that "All things being equal, rich is better." But it is important to note that neither money, nor the things that money will buy, make us happy. Happiness is an internal thermostat that we set ourselves. Abraham Lincoln, someone who was plagued his whole life with clinical depression, said, "People are about as happy as they decide to be."

Most people are running faster and pushing harder to get more. Too often, they are performing a job they don't enjoy for people they don't respect to get things to impress others who simply don't care. If you were to probe these striving individuals in search of more, at some point they would tell you they are doing this for their family. Let's examine your net worth versus your net value as it relates to your family.

1. Think of the people in your ancestry who have impacted your life and the way you live the most. You will probably discover these high-impact people left you life values instead of money.

2. Think of the people in your past who impacted you during your formative years. You will likely determine that they invested time, love, and lessons into your life—not just capital.

3. Think of the special times with friends and family that meant the most to you then and now. You will probably realize that these occasions may have been low-cost or no-cost events.

4. What are you leaving to your heirs in the way of time, lessons, and memories? If you're trading these things in for the pursuit of more, you may be spending the most valuable part of their inheritance without their permission. They want you, not just your money.

Like most life lessons, this one is a balancing act. We human beings seek black-and-white answers to gray questions. Nothing will replace money in the things that money does, but beyond that point, nothing will replace you in the hearts, minds, and spirits of the special people in your life.

As you go through your day today, find ways to increase both your net worth and your net value for those you love.

Today's the day!

4

Wealth 101

I wrote the following column nearly 20 years ago in response to many questions from people around the world seeking the magic bullet or secret formula to becoming a millionaire. The reality of becoming a millionaire is so simple that most people miss it. You have to spend less than you earn. There are only two sides to this equation, so we are all left with the fact that we have to spend less, earn more, or work both sides of that equation at the same time.

While economic conditions may have shifted since people read this column in newspapers, magazines, and online publications around the world, the fundamentals remain the same.

Yesterday I heard a statistic that is tremendously significant. The first impression of this statistic was so insignificant that I almost didn't get it. Then the true import of what I was hearing dawned on me. Last month, the national average savings rate

> The reality of becoming a millionaire is so simple—you have to spend less than you earn.

was a negative 1%. At first glance, 1% doesn't seem like a big number, and the fact that it only deals with the savings rate doesn't seem to indicate an immediate crisis. However, there are some facts in play here that we need to understand.

Interest rates are still at a historic low that most of us have not experienced in our lifetimes.

Our economy is relatively healthy and growing at a good pace. Employment is approaching a level we would consider full employment. And, overall, the economic outlook is pretty good. The last time we had a negative 1% savings rate nationally was in 1933. This, our fans of history will remember, was the low point of the Great Depression; therefore, this begs the question: "What's going to happen if things get really bad?"

This is probably a good point for you and me to review the myths and realities of wealth building.

The greatest myth about wealthy people is that they either inherited the money or won the lottery. In reality, over 90% of millionaires are first-generation millionaires who earned, saved, and invested their own money. People who win the lottery are more likely to file bankruptcy in the following 10 years than the average working-class person in our society. Therefore, with respect to wealth building, we must rely on the old adage: *"If it is to be, it is up to me."*

Now that we've dispelled the myths and established personal responsibility, let's go over a few rules for building our wealth.

1. Spend less than you earn.

2. Avoid borrowing money.

3. Live on a budget.

4. Save and invest regularly.

This would seem to be an elementary school explanation of wealth building. In reality, many millionaires in our society only have an elementary school education. If you're going to win any game, you first need to understand the rules, then follow the lead of those who have already won. Whether I am writing books, speaking from the platform, or putting together these weekly columns, probably my best advice ever is, "Don't take advice from anybody who doesn't have what you want." This certainly applies as you strive to reach your financial goals.

As you go through your day today, remember the simple rules of wealth building and apply them to your life. They are, indeed, simple but not easy. If it were easy, everyone would be rich.

Today's the day!

5

Money Myths

When I wrote *The Millionaire Map* about my own journey from poverty to prosperity, I put together a Millionaire Map Assessment that people can fill out. It is designed to reveal beliefs, misunderstandings, and prejudices that could affect their pursuit of becoming a millionaire. If you would like to take the Millionaire Map Assessment yourself, it's available for you at this link: https://www.jimstovall.com/millionaire-map-assessment.

If you're one of those misguided individuals I wrote about in the following column who believes money is evil and millionaires are dishonest, greedy, manipulative people, it will be very difficult for you to actively pursue building wealth with the focus and intensity that is required.

Money is probably the most misunderstood commodity in the history of humanity. While it is not the most important thing in life, nothing can take the place of money in the things that money does. If we are to understand money and use it properly, we must dispel the old and deeply ingrained money myths.

1. Money will make you happy. All one needs to do to prove this to be false is to look at the entertainment news and see how much heartbreak, divorce, and suicide play a part in the lives of the rich and famous. Money will certainly not make you happy, but neither will poverty. It is important to have just enough money to reach all of the goals and dreams we have.

2. Some people are lucky when it comes to money. No one other than those who work in a mint make money. All money is earned. Money is earned by labor or by money earning additional money. Even if you hear about someone who has been given money, always remember someone earned that money or it was derived via investment. If you want to have more money, learn how to create more value in the lives of others, and the money will follow.

3. Money is evil. Money is absolutely neutral. It is not good or bad. Like a gun, knife, or any other tool, it can be used to any end. The most horrible atrocities and the most wonderful blessings ever known have been facilitated by money.

4. Average people cannot get ahead. There are more millionaires being created today than ever before. They are not born as millionaires. They simply find a way to create enough value in the lives of people so that they are rewarded financially. Compound interest should be known globally as The Eighth Wonder

Love people and use money.

of the World. Most people understand exchanging their time and effort for money. What millionaires understand is that money will begat more money if it is saved and invested wisely. No one ever borrowed their way to financial independence. You must get on the positive side of the compound interest wave.

Examine your financial goals and the vehicles you are using to reach them. Take all the emotion out of the money game and use it as a tool. Always remember to love people and use money. If you get this backwards, you are destined to fail no matter how much you have.

As you go through your day today, make sure your money works for you and the things you care about.

Today's the day!

6

Boring Is Best

As you read the following column, it's important to remember that while I advocate everybody becoming a millionaire through time-tested, boring methods, I also believe in amassing great wealth through entrepreneurship by creating tremendous value in the marketplace. I have never had a traditional job as I have always chosen to work for myself. As a blind person, I fit better into an environment that I create and control.

Entrepreneurship has created financial success in my life beyond my wildest dreams, but in the midst of my ventures, I've always invested in stable retirement funds, and I have become a millionaire through the boring means I recommend for everyone else.

Wealth has enabled me to get involved in philanthropy. Among our many giving projects, we founded the Stovall Center for Entrepreneurships at Oral Roberts University. Students from around the world come to earn their degrees and learn how to start businesses, create wealth, and change the world. In my first lecture to the new students each year, as I'm encouraging them to reach for the stars, I also remind them not to miss the basics and be committed to becoming a millionaire the boring way while they are lighting the fuse of innovation and cutting-edge technology that will change the world in the future.

Recently, I was on a flight into Chicago to speak at an arena event. I always enjoy these trips because they give me the opportunity to actually meet a number of people who read these columns, enjoy the programming we produce at Narrative Television Network, or have seen *The Ultimate Gift* movie which is based on one of my books.

I ate a nice meal on the plane and was enjoying a smooth and comfortable flight. At one point, the pilot emerged from the cockpit, and we got into a conversation. He inquired about my travels, and I let him know that I was really excited about my trip. Then I asked him how the flight was going up front in the cockpit, and he told me that it was boring as usual. After a bit more conversation, we both agreed that the best travel involves a boring flight and an exciting trip.

While most everyone would agree that boring flights are best, the majority of people do not adhere to these principles where it relates to their financial life. Many people are approaching retirement, and they are going to have a boring retirement because they decided to have an exciting investment plan.

People who like exciting investment plans fail to diversify because they want to invest all of their capital in the latest hot stock or can't-miss real estate deal. These same people see no need to invest regularly because they are going to strike it rich somewhere down the road. These investors who crave excitement fail to begin saving and investing when they're young because they would rather invest their money in exciting consumer goods and mounting credit card debt.

On the other hand, if you want to win financially, think boring. If you avoid consumer debt and invest as little as $50 per week throughout your working life in a conservative portfolio or index fund, you may be bored as you read your steadily growing monthly statements, but you will assuredly retire a multimillionaire, therefore insuring an exciting life. Remember, retirement is not an age, it's an amount of money. Once your money earns as much or more than you do, you no longer have to work to make a living. Retirement doesn't mean you sit around and do nothing. It means you get to select your pursuits from the endless smorgasbord that life has to offer.

> Become a millionaire the boring way, while lighting the fuse of innovation and cutting-edge technology to change the future.

As you go through your day today, remember to keep your flights and financial planning boring. Therefore, your trips and your life can be tremendously exciting.

Today's the day!

7

Do It Yourself

You may have noticed that each of the columns that make up the sections of this book end with the phrase, "Today's the day." I have used that phrase at the end of my weekly columns for more than 25 years because I want to remind my readers in newspapers, magazines, and online publications around the world that it doesn't matter what we meant to do, intended to do, knew to do, or if we regretted what we didn't do. All that matters is what we actually did. We must accept the reality that we are in our present financial condition because of the choices we've made in the past. Only when we accept full responsibility for all that has gone before, can we take control of all that's coming in the future.

We all recognize that which we call success is a do-it-yourself project. It is easy to identify the self-made millionaire, start-up entrepreneur, or others who started with nothing and achieved their own goals. While none of us succeed without the constant

> *It doesn't matter what we meant to do, intended to do, knew to do, or if we regretted what we didn't do. All that matters is what we actually did.*

support, encouragement, and cooperation of others, we can all identify the self-directed nature of success. Failure is much harder to account for. As normal human beings, we have the tendency to take credit for our successes and assign blame for our failures.

In the world where we live, move, and have our being today, it is easier than ever to achieve whatever your idea of success might be. There are more millionaires and, indeed, billionaires created every day than at any point in recorded history. More people are creating lives and lifestyles so that they can successfully live life on their own terms and according to their own definition of success.

With the potential opportunity scale slanted in our favor, one of the most important elements of becoming successful is to simply avoid failure. Most ventures that fail do so because they simply did not have the staying power. The proverbial plant died before it had an opportunity to bear fruit. In many cases, these mortal wounds are self-inflicted. We must avoid, at all cost, the things that will take us out of the game before we have an opportunity to win.

If you want to succeed in business or in your personal finances, the following are a few failure pitfalls to avoid:

1. Have a personal and business financial plan that involves a significant cash reserve for all contingencies.

2. Insurance premiums are cheap compared to the catastrophic losses you may face. If you can't afford the insurance, you certainly won't survive that which you are failing to insure against.

3. Consistently withhold and promptly pay your taxes. We all have an Uncle Sam who is not going to wait for his money regardless of your current financial crisis.

4. Accelerate income and defer expenses as long as possible. Time is, indeed, money. You need all the time you can get, and cash will provide it for you.

5. Keep your eye on the ball and make sure it's your own ball. It's too easy to get distracted and run down a rabbit trail that offers you a clear path directly to somewhere you don't want to be.

As you go through your day today, remember that both success and failure are do-it-yourself propositions. Avoid failure and keep working, and success will be yours.

Today's the day!

8

Insuring Your Future

I remember attending an event for accredited investors after achieving multimillionaire status. To be an accredited investor, you must have a large income, a high net worth, or both. I remember the host of the event opened his remarks by saying, "This is not a get-rich meeting, this is a stay-rich meeting." While it's not always fun and exciting, you must give some thought to protecting the wealth you're building.

You can spend a lifetime creating value in the world that results in you becoming a millionaire, and you can lose it or have it taken from you very quickly if you don't take a few simple, easy steps.

We would all like to live a risk-free, stress-free life. Unfortunately, this is not available to us here in the 21st century. We simply have to weigh the risks we face, accept those we can manage, and insure ourselves against those we cannot afford. Most consumer experts tell us that buying extended warranties on electronics and mechanical items is generally not worthwhile. These products have basically become disposable and are obsolete in a few short years or even sooner. If you can afford to repair or replace them on your own, avoid paying for extended coverage, as it is extremely expensive compared to the price of the item it covers.

When it comes to your home or your car, you will want to have adequate coverage. You can save quite a bit of money by raising the deductible on your home policy, which simply means you would have to pay the first $1,000 or even $2,000 of any claim. Often, you can afford to pay these deductibles out of the premium savings you have achieved by raising the deductible on your policies.

Once you start to accumulate wealth and achieve financial independence, as I hope all of my readers will do, you need to look at having an umbrella insurance policy. It covers you in the case of liability or lawsuits not covered by any of your other policies. For example, if you are in a tragic car accident in which another driver is severely injured, the liability can run into millions of dollars. A standard automobile policy would only pay a fraction of this, and you would be forced to cover the rest. This incident is where an umbrella policy would step in to secure your wealth and financial future.

> While you can't avoid all risks, you can minimize the big ones and manage the small ones.

Recently, I discovered a wonderful free tool that can assist you if you've had a close friend, colleague, or family member pass away. They could have had a life insurance policy naming you as the beneficiary without you even knowing about it. You fill out a brief online form at https://eapps.naic.org/life-policy-locator/#/welcome, and they will search every major insurance company for policies relating to the individual you listed and let you know if you are the beneficiary. This site worked very well for me after the recent death of a family member.

While you can't avoid all risks, you can minimize the big ones and manage the small ones.

As you go through your day today, protect everything you have worked so hard for.

Today's the day!

9

Driving Your Money

When I wrote this *Winners' Wisdom* column in 2007, I had not imagined that I would include Will Rogers as a character in one of my novels and that *Will to Win* would be in production as a movie as I am compiling this book. Will's words are more true today than they were nearly a century ago, and the statistics I site in the following column have become more alarming throughout the ensuing years.

When you realize that a few hundred dollars a month invested wisely throughout your working life can make you a millionaire, the foolishness of a car payment comes into clear focus.

Among the most profound philosophers and columnists of the 20th-century was Will Rogers. People waited each day to learn what Will would write in the newspaper or say on the radio. During the depths of the Depression, he announced, "America will go down in history as the only nation that will go to the poor house in an automobile." That was true then and maybe even more profound today.

The average car payment in America is approaching $400 per month over 72 months. This virtually ensures that most of the cars driving on the highway will never be paid off. There will be a remaining balance when that car is traded in on a new one, and the remaining debt is rolled into a new loan. When you consider that cars are the most expensive things we buy that go down in value, this is a recipe for disaster.

When you study millionaires, you find that—on average—they drive a two- to three-year-old car and keep it for a number of years. Paying cash for a two- to three-year-old car allows you to enjoy a very nice automobile while letting someone else take the depreciation hit that happens within the first few years after a car drives away from the show room.

If the average car payment, $400 per month, were invested over a working lifetime, you, your children, and grandchildren could be financially independent. If you can ever get to the point where you make that last payment on your car, don't consider it the end but consider it the beginning. Continue to drive that car and continue to make the monthly payment, but instead of paying the finance company, pay yourself. Within a few short years, you will have the ability to act like the average millionaire in our society when you walk onto a car lot and pay cash for your next automobile. If you will continue making these payments to yourself instead of making the payments plus interest to the bank, you will be on your way to financial success. Don't buy into the myth that you have to have a car payment for your entire life.

Nothing rides better than a paid-for car.

We are bombarded with car ads offering us easy terms, no money down, and liberal trade-in opportunities. If it seems like this is a great deal, it is, but only if you're a bank or automobile finance company. Nothing rides better than a paid-for car.

As you go through your day today, think of your car in terms of your long-term financial planning and not your response to a short-term TV ad.

Today's the day!

10

Wall Street on Sale

I began my business career as an investment broker for a New York Stock Exchange member firm. During the 1980s, we did not have all the digital access to the market we enjoy today. Instantaneous stock quotes did not exist. Unfortunately, for most investors, the 21st-century technology intended to assist in building wealth has too often provided a window to worry about the value of their portfolio.

We don't often worry about the value of our homes or cars because those valuations are not flashed in our faces multiple times every day. There are many times when your home, which is likely one of your largest assets, is going down in value. But if you don't know it, you comfortably ride through the dips and enjoy the growth of your equity. Most everyone realizes that the value of their car is going down every day, but there aren't instantaneous quotes reminding us of the decline.

The stock market may seem like a roller coaster, but the only people who get injured are those who jump off.

I am certainly not the first to tell you that the way to make money in the stock market is to buy low and sell high. As ridiculously simple as this seems, the majority of individual investors make a habit of buying high and selling low. This is because they invest with their heart and not with their head.

> The stock market may seem like a roller coaster, but the only people who get injured are those who jump off.

You can visualize the stock market by picturing a young boy walking upstairs playing with a yo-yo. If you focus on the boy ascending the stairs, you will be very comfortable. If you focus, however, on the quick, abrupt drops of the yo-yo, you will panic.

Everyone seems to have a good attitude when the market is up, but to an average individual investor, a down market signals distress, depression, and doom. To the successful, long-term investor, a down market signals a buying opportunity. It's like going to the mall when everything is on sale. When you consider these buying opportunities, it is realistic to think that you make money when you buy and not just when you sell.

There are a few things to keep in mind if you are going to invest in the stock market:

1. Diversify. You must own a wide number of stocks from a diverse number of industries. If you put all your eggs in one basket, you may do well this month and this year, but you are a disaster waiting to happen. There are a number of index funds and mutual funds for small investors who do not have the resources to diversify on their own.

2. Have a long-term horizon. If you cannot invest your money for more than five years, do not invest in the stock market. Remember the boy with the yo-yo. Over a five-year period or longer, it's easy to have results that look like the boy climbing the stairs; however, if you have a short-term horizon, it is likely your results will look like the yo-yo when the bottom drops out.

3. Invest regularly. Most investors succeed when they have a systematic, automatic, regular investment plan. They put money into selected investments at the same time each month or each quarter. This makes it more likely you will be investing with your head and not your heart.

4. Don't get married to any single investment. Remember, we want to buy low and sell high—not buy low, watch it get high, and then become low again. When you buy a stock, you should already have your sell point in mind. Look at everything

in your portfolio and consider if you didn't own it, would you buy it. If the answer is not an emphatic "Yes," sell today.

As you go through your day today, look at your investments as a long-term vehicle taking you toward your dreams. Short-term drops in the market simply signal a blue-light special.

Today's the day!

Money will never change who you are, but it will make you more of whatever you are right now.

11

Good and Evil

Some of the issues that impact people seeking to build wealth or become a millionaire are constant. I wrote the following column recently, but it addresses issues that have been prevalent among my readers for over a quarter of a century. We cannot outrun or outperform our world view, but we can have what my late, great friend and colleague Dr. Stephen Covey called a "paradigm shift."

If you've ever been in the audience at one of the arena events or business conventions where I speak, you have likely heard me say, *"You change your life when you change your mind."*

Money is a result, not a cause. Money comes to us when we create value in the lives of other people. Too many people are focused on having the things they perceive that millionaires have. Before you have those things, you have to do the things that millionaires do. And before you can do those things, you have to be the person who can create that value.

We are not human *havings* or human *doings*. We are human *beings*. Once we get the millionaire mindset, we will do the right things and have everything we want.

◆———◆———◆

For over a quarter century, I have received countless questions from people around the world who regularly read this weekly *Winners' Wisdom* column in newspapers, magazines, or in online publications. The one topic more people inquire about than any other is building wealth and how to become a millionaire.

First and foremost, the foundation for becoming a millionaire is based upon your perception of wealth and people who acquire it. Many of us grew up hearing repeated messages in school, church, or the media telling us that money is the root of evil. This deceptive falsehood comes from an ancient scripture that proclaims, "The love of money is the root of all evil." That is a powerful message and a wonderful reminder for people building wealth and aspiring to live as a millionaire. We should all love people and use money as a tool to do the things in our lives that matter most to us and those we serve.

Your perception of money is vitally important as you progress toward your goal of becoming a millionaire. If you had a goal to take an extended trip to live and travel in a distant country, your success would be greatly dependent upon what you think of that country and the people who live there. If you have internalized repeated messages telling you it's a horrible place to be and it's inhabited by terrible people, I question how hard you will work and how diligent you will be on your quest to get there.

> ## You hold the future in your hand.

Money will never change who you are, but it will make you more of whatever you are right now. If you are a loving, giving person who wants to make a difference in the world, money can make that happen in tangible and significant ways. On the other hand, if you are a manipulative, vindictive, or destructive person, a large amount of money will make it possible for you to spread your poison to more people around the world.

It puts me in mind of the fable about the teenage boy who approached the wise man in his village. The young man had caught a bird which he was holding in his hand, and he wanted to trick the wise man, so he asked, "Is this bird living or dead?" The wise man spoke to the boy as he speaks to us today saying, "If I say the bird is dead, you will open your hand and let it fly away. If I say the bird is living, you will squeeze the life out of it. So as in most things, life and death as well as good and evil is in your hands."

Becoming a millionaire can be the best thing that ever happened to you or the worst thing imaginable for everyone around you. You hold the future in your hand.

As you go through your day today, remember that your money will mirror your life and be used for good or evil.

Today's the day!

12

When Money Matters

Whether you are planning to become a millionaire through entrepreneurship or investments, you will need to know the basics of how to run a business and evaluate finances. Entrepreneurs start businesses, and investors invest in ongoing businesses. It is often hard to know how to capitalize a venture.

I have written more than 50 books and, to date, nine of them have been turned into movies. Making a motion picture is a great way to hemorrhage money. Millions of dollars are spent taking the ideas from my novels and turning them into movies. I always ask my financial partners or producers of the films the question, "How much of the cash we're spending is going to end up on the screen?"

While it's great to invest resources in your final product, it's easy to get caught up in the folly of trying to build value with things that don't really matter. I wrote this column over 15 years ago using my own business as an example. I believe it will benefit you as you create your own venture or invest in others.

All of us who are in business face the constant struggle of knowing when to spend money and when not to. Money can be the fuel that takes your business to the next level, or it can be the ball and chain that drags you down to oblivion. There are many choices in how we spend or invest our business capital. Some of these expenditures matter, and others don't. Understanding the difference can give you an edge on your competition and make you stable and successful.

> It's easy to get caught up in the folly of trying to build value with things that don't really matter.

My core business, the Narrative Television Network, makes movies and television accessible for 13 million blind and visually impaired Americans and their families. We provide extra soundtracks to all of the major broadcast and cable networks.

Our clients are huge multinational, upscale corporations; however, we are in our 20th year of doing business with a myriad of these types of clients and not one of them has ever set foot in our offices and studios. All our work is done by phone, mail, email, etc. Therefore, as we consider how to make our money matter, we have determined to have very nice and functional offices and studios but present our corporate image through mail, email, website, etc.

I cannot tell you how many times I have gone into new startup businesses that are similar to ours in that they do not interact with their clients in their facilities. Too often, I find that these struggling businesses have wasted many thousands of dollars in furniture and equipment that does not affect their performance or bottom line. Our company has actually acquired slightly used furniture and equipment on occasion from these overextended companies as they go out of business.

Deciding when the money really matters is an individual question, so I can't give you the specific answers for your organization, but I can give you some questions to ponder before you spend money.

1. What is the direct and indirect benefit to our organization if I spend this money?

2. What is the worst thing that can happen if I avoid or delay spending this money?

3. What is the image I want my company to have to customers, vendors, and others with whom we interact?

4. Who can I ask for an honest, independent opinion of the current image we portray?

5. What expenditures and opportunities do we have coming up in the short and medium term that may require capital?

6. Is there a way to acquire this equipment, furniture, or material without spending cash now?

As you go through your day today, remember: Money matters, but don't waste it on things you don't need to impress people who don't care.

Today's the day!

13

The Perfect Investment

As you begin your quest to build wealth and become a millionaire, it's important to realize that, in the beginning, most of the dollars you will accumulate will come from your own work. Later in the process, your money will work for you and generate amazing returns. I am at the height of my professional career and can generate more income than ever before in my working life. However, regardless of what I do or don't do, my accumulated wealth generates more money for me every day than I can earn through my own efforts.

Investing is a very specialized, rapidly changing field filled with many people who want your business. There's nothing more valuable than the right investment professional, and there is nothing more harmful than the wrong one. You will first want to vet your investment advisor by asking for a number of references, and then you will want to follow up on every one of them. You should never invest in anything that you don't fully understand, so it is vital that your investment advisor is able to communicate effectively.

If I go to the doctor, I don't want to have to attend medical school to understand his or her diagnosis. Whether it's replacing your muffler, landscaping your property, or fixing one of your appliances, we all deal with people who perform tasks that we do not have the knowledge or skill to perform.

You should never invest in anything that you don't fully understand.

You want to find an investment professional who has already created wealth for themselves and many clients.

As a success speaker, columnist, and author, many people assume I have the secret answer to every question. Nothing could be farther from the truth. One of the questions I am asked more than any other is "What is the best investment?" Asking about the best investment is like asking "What's the best thing to order for dinner?" or "What's the best size of shoe to buy?" The right answer is, quite simply, "It depends."

All of us invest every dollar we have. Some dollars are invested in stocks, bonds, and commodities, while others are invested in cars, boats, vacations, and items at the mall. Any or all of these are appropriate ways to utilize your money in the right way and at the right time. If you are a 25-year-old starting your first job and wondering where to invest your retirement funds, my advice would be quite different from if you are 60 years old and planning to retire in the next four or five years.

All investments offer one or more of the three basic characteristics of what I call the Investment Triangle. Imagine an equilateral triangle with the three points labeled Safety, Liquidity, and Return. Every investment vehicle will fall somewhere within that triangle. The closer you get to one point of the triangle, the farther you will move from the other two points.

Therefore, an investment that offers a very high return will have a lower degree of safety or liquidity. An investment that is totally safe may have a poor return or not be liquid. An investment that is available to you at any time will be liquid but may have a very low yield. A good investment is an investment that simply meets your needs. Everyone should have some money invested for safety, liquidity, and return at all times.

Everyone should strive to be completely out of consumer debt and have six months' worth of living expenses in a totally safe account that can be accessed at any time. This should be accomplished before any other non-retirement investments are made. If you have no consumer debt, have six months of living expenses set aside, and are regularly funding your retirement, I want to be the first to welcome you to the top 10% of investors. You have passed 90% of people before you purchase your first stock, bond, or mutual fund outside of your retirement account.

As you go through your day today, before you move on to exotic high-profile investments, remember to take care of the basics.

Today's the day!

14

Financial Intelligence

I wrote the following column in 2008, which was a very disruptive and difficult time in the financial world. The column was written in response to many inquiries based on false information. Many people mistakenly believe that to become a millionaire you must inherit money, be extremely lucky, or somehow cheat the system. In reality, the vast majority of millionaires are honest, first-generation people of wealth who have acquired money the slow and steady way, which is how the tortoise beat the hare.

As you are acquiring knowledge and financial intelligence, always remember it's an ongoing process not a singular event. The financial realm is changing so rapidly that you have to be a lifelong learner to permanently enjoy wealth in the 21st century.

◆——◆——◆

For years, academic experts have been measuring people's intelligence by administering an I.Q. test. More recently, behavioral scientists and those in the field of psychology have been discussing a principle they call emotional intelligence. I would submit there is another intellectual area of expertise I would call financial intelligence.

Financial intelligence would not measure how smart you are or even how learned you have become. Instead, financial intelligence would measure your mastery of some basic concepts, the application of which creates financial success. Financial intelligence is far different from general intelligence. Some of the people who are known as among the smartest individuals in the world are at or near bankruptcy. Albert Einstein lost almost all the money he received as a part of his Nobel Prize through bad investments.

Money is not what makes us wealthy. Money is simply the result of applying certain principles that might make up financial intelligence. If you divided all the money equally among everyone, in a few short years, the wealth landscape would look much like it does today. Therefore, we understand that money is not wealth. It is the result of applying financial intelligence in the real world.

There are at least as many financial success systems as there are financial planners and money experts; but there are a few principles that seem to appear consistently in the

> **Financial intelligence measures your mastery of basic concepts; the application creates financial success.**

lives, careers, and investments of those we would call financially successful. If you want to be more financially successful or conduct your own financial intelligence checkup, consider the following:

1. Do you have a financial goal that belongs to you, or are you trying to keep up with the proverbial Joneses?

2. Do you have a budget or an overall understanding of where your money is currently going?

3. Are you consistently saving for your retirement, and do you understand that, statistically, you will need to take care of yourself for decades without a significant safety net?

4. Have you eliminated all of your consumer debt? You cannot succeed if you are paying both principle and interest on things that are no longer here or are not worth what you owe on them.

5. Do you have a will and insurance to take care of all the potential disasters in your family's life?

6. Do you understand that each dollar should be divided among three categories—spending, saving, and giving?

As you go through your day today, remember that knowledge, wisdom, and expertise are not necessarily transferable. You may know a lot about many things, but your financial future will be governed by your financial intelligence.

Today's the day!

15

The Value of Money

This column was written in response to many questions from readers based on the false premise that money will solve every problem in life. Money is a tool. It is only helpful in the areas where money is required, then it is indispensable. Money will not, in and of itself, make you happy, healthy, or create wonderful relationships among your family and friends.

News reports abound of mega-wealthy people who are depressed and suicidal. Laboring for years under the impression that money is a panacea, then arriving at millionaire status only to find that money alone can create an empty, hollow existence is an ongoing theme.

If you have goals and dreams that can be accomplished with money, becoming a millionaire may fulfill all your desires. But simply having a bank account or investment portfolio with a lot of zeros is futile.

Money will not make you happy. I hasten to add that neither will poverty make you happy. In a recent study on happiness, it was determined that, beyond basic food, clothing, and shelter (approximately $50K annual income in the U.S.) adding more money to the equation did not necessarily make one

> Money will not, in and of itself, make you happy, healthy, or create wonderful relationships among your family and friends.

happy. Money without purpose is like fuel without a destination. It is useless if not dangerous to have around if you don't have a purpose.

At a time when I had written a dozen books, I will never forget the day when an eminent financial planner and estate attorney called me to compliment me on my book on finance. He said he had given over 1,000 of the books away, and he wanted me to know how much the book meant to him. I was flattered but baffled at the same time. I was glad that one of my books had found meaning in his life and in the lives of the clients he served; however, I wasn't aware that I had written a book on financial planning or estate planning.

When he told me he was referring to my book *The Ultimate Gift*, I had to stop and think about why that book was considered by this imminent professional to be a breakthrough in estate and financial planning. *The Ultimate Gift* and the subsequent movie from 20th Century Fox based on the book, is a story about life, principles, goals, and values. Money is not the major theme of *The Ultimate Gift*, the three sequel books, or movie trilogy. I only used a billionaire character in the stories to try to put money into perspective. Then I realized the ultimate lesson about money is not about money. It's about life. The lesson is as personal and individualized as you and me.

We cannot do planning by looking at a financial statement any more than we could fit you with the perfect pair of shoes by talking to you on the telephone. Always remember, when you're talking to a financial planner, a lawyer, a CPA, insurance professional, banker, or anyone else you call upon to help you with your financial plan, the most they can accomplish is to make your money do what you want it to in the context of your life. Letting them drive your future is like letting the gas station attendant tell you where to drive your car. Resources without direction, wealth without planning, and money without destiny is the height of human folly.

As you go through your day today, remember that unlimited money and the best advice in the world will not help you unless you know where you want to go and what you want to do.

Today's the day!

16

Living and Retiring

Among the many treasures of wisdom I received from my grandmother is the statement, "Don't wish your life away." When we're children it's easy to want it to be summer when we're in school, then we can't wait until football season starts in the fall or the Christmas holiday approaches. While all of these events are wonderful, we need to experience every day as the gift that it is.

As the author of more than 50 books, I'm embarrassed to admit to you that, when I could read with my eyes as you are reading the words on this page, I never really read at all. After losing my sight, I discovered audiobooks and got involved with highspeed, compressed digital audio listening. The result of this is that, for more than 30 years, I have read an entire book every day. Being a reader made me want to be a writer. I've read countless books about a myriad of topics.

Several years ago, I read more than a dozen titles about people who climbed Mount Everest. It was interesting to learn that climbing the tallest mountain in the world can literally take several years to organize, fund, and mount an expedition in hopes that the weather and other climbing variables will give you a brief window of opportunity to reach the summit. A recurring theme among the Mount Everest books is the thought that you have to enjoy the journey because, at best, you may spend a few short minutes on the top of the world.

Retirement may be your golden years, and it is well worth planning for, but don't wish away today and miss the magic planning for tomorrow.

◆――――◆――――◆

To the vast majority of people who populate this planet today and to virtually everyone who has populated this planet since the beginning of time, the concept of retirement would be unknown.

Retirement is not an age. It is, instead, an amount of money. It is important to realize that retirement funds do not exist so you can afford to do nothing. Retirement funds exist so you can afford to do anything and everything you want to do with your life. Money only exists to give us choices. This does not change because you have crossed some imaginary age barrier at 65, 67, or 70.

Before you contemplate your future, which is uncertain at best, please first contemplate today. All of us have one important day that we deal with. It is not the day we retire. It is the day we're living right now. If you do not enjoy your life, your career, your leisure time, and every other aspect of your existence, you need to start making some changes now. Don't become a part of the growing herd of people who are willing to trade quiet desperation today for a fairytale existence somewhere in the nebulous future.

> **Don't trade quiet desperation today for a fairytale existence somewhere in the nebulous future.**

My father runs one of the larger retirement homes in the city where I live. He and my mother work very hard to help people adjust to their retirement years. It is interesting to note, as my father approaches his 78th birthday, that while being around retired people all day every day, he chooses to continue to work. He does not work because he needs the money, as my mother and father could have retired decades ago with more than enough money to live their lives as they choose. The irony is that they continue to work because they are living their lives the way they choose.

Obviously, I echo the thoughts of most financial planners that proper financial planning for retirement is essential. This planning should never be undertaken with the thought that, with enough money, you could buy your way out of servitude in a job or career you hate. Retirement financial planning should be looked upon as a way to continue to live your life the way you have always lived your life as a happy, fulfilled, contented person making a difference in the world around you.

Several years ago, I became aware of a husband and wife who had diligently worked for decades, scrimping and hoarding enough money so they could retire in their mid-50s. As the magic date approached for their retirement, they were like long-term prison inmates with a parole date approaching. They gleefully planned their retirement party that would be followed by a luxury cruise for which they had saved for many years.

Tragically, just a few months before the retirement party and the luxury cruise into their sunset years of retirement, the wife died of cancer leaving the husband to face an unknown future with non-existent hopes and dreams for which he had sacrificed throughout his most productive years.

As you plan for tomorrow, be sure you don't forget to live for today. Your past is a cancelled check that you can do nothing about. Your future is a promissory note filled with doubt and mystery. Your present life that you are living today is cash. Spend it wisely, and don't miss the boat.

Today's the day!

17

The Life of Money

Throughout the years, I've received so many calls and emails about people's money goals that I felt compelled to write this column. Having a goal that is represented by an amount of money is like setting an objective to have a quantity of gasoline instead of proactively planning your family's vacation. We all have deeply held dreams and aspirations. These are magnificent things we want to be, do, and have in our lifetime. Money is a component in some of those goals, but it is not a valid destination all by itself.

Ralph Waldo Emerson said, "There's nothing capricious in nature." Emerson meant that the world around us will never trick or fool us. If you have a lofty goal, dream, or ambition, you have the capacity to achieve it and can obtain the money needed to live out your destiny. The dream would not have been put inside of you if you did not have the capacity to achieve it. So, the question is never, "Can we?" The question is, "Will we?"

> **If you have a lofty goal, dream, or ambition, you have the capacity to achieve it and can obtain the money needed to live out your destiny.**

Money is probably the most misunderstood commodity in our society. People today understand the price of everything and the value of nothing. There have been more conflicts, divorces, and disputes over money than anything else. In order to begin to have healthy attitudes toward money, we must understand that it is nothing more or less than a tool or a vehicle. Money can get us what we want or take us where we want to go. Unless there is something you want or somewhere you wish to go, money has no value.

How would your life be different if money were no object? This is a difficult question to consider because we seldom make any decisions that are not based upon money. This is a poor way to look at the world. Decide what is good or right or meaningful, and then worry about the money.

You may be interested to know there has never been a money shortage. There is, however, from time to time a creativity, service, or value shortage. Money is nothing more or less than a result of creating value in the lives of other people. If you stop worrying about money and start worrying about creating value in the lives of those around you, you will have more money than you need. If you simply worry about money, you will never have enough.

You will be like the foolish person standing in front of the stove saying, "Give me heat, and then I will give you wood."

The life of money is just one of the twelve gifts featured in the movie based on my novel *The Ultimate Life*. *The Ultimate Life* and the life of money teach us that everything we need to live out our biggest dreams and our ultimate destiny has already been provided for us. I hope you will begin to utilize the life of money and make money your servant instead of being a slave to it. I hope you will watch *The Ultimate Life* movie and begin to see your life unfold as the fulfillment of your biggest dreams and your ultimate destiny.

As you go through your day today, remember money can fuel your vehicle to transport you to your ultimate life.

Today's the day!

18

Magical Money

Over a decade ago, I wrote the "Magical Money" column in response to people's ongoing false impressions that we can somehow manage or manipulate our money to reach our goals. The concept of managing time or money is folly. There will always be 24 hours in a day and 100 cents in a dollar. What we have to manage is ourselves, our habits, and our behavior. We don't fail because we don't know what to do. We fail because we don't do what we know.

Everyone who lights up a cigarette today is fully aware that the pack the cigarette came from clearly warns them of the health hazards. If they don't believe they can defeat reality, they certainly act as if they can delay it. When you understand the time value of money, not acting prudently will cost you a great deal.

If you have 30 years until retirement, your money will act like a snowball rolling downhill. The closer it gets to the end, the bigger the snowball gets and the faster it accelerates. The final year of your 30-year financial plan will yield an extraordinary amount of money. If you procrastinate another 12 months, you will be missing that amazing financial return at the end of your journey. All of my columns end with the phrase, "Today's the day," but it's particularly poignant at the end of this message.

There are few things in our chaotic lives that are more reliable and dependable than money. Dollars can be counted, budgeted, and allocated. Money acts the same way every time and will do exactly what you tell it to do, but it's not magic. I'm always amazed when people take this down-to-earth medium of exchange and expect it to be magical.

> We don't fail because we don't know what to do. We fail because we don't do what we know.

For over 25 years, I have had a college scholarship, and to date, we have helped send over 500 students to my alma mater. Recently, I ran into an aspiring student and her mother at an event where I was speaking. They told me they were hoping to get one of my scholarships. When I told them we were going to have a board meeting to review the scholarships in just a few days they were astonished and replied, "Oh, we didn't fill out an application."

I am baffled how often people expect their bills to be paid, retirement to be established, and expenses to be handled through some magical property of money that simply doesn't exist. If you're depending on money to do something that can't be added up, multiplied, or compounded, it's probably not going to happen. People are invariably waiting for their ship to come in, and the majority of them never sent a ship out.

A significant percentage of people who have access to free matching dollars for their retirement funds through their employer still don't take advantage of it. People who attend my *Millionaire Institute* events learn that if you will save $10 a day and invest in a simple Index Fund that has returned 12% for more than half a century, you will be a millionaire in 30 years. People are astonished when they see the simple mathematics, but when I follow up to see how many of them are saving $10 a day, I am generally disappointed by people's failure to engage.

Money is a great tool if you use it and a tremendous slave if you will put it to work. Money is the fuel that can make your dreams come true, but they will always be just dreams if you don't put the fuel in the engine and engage the ignition switch. To end up where you want to be, you have to go on a journey from here to there, and to have a successful journey, you have to start. Financial independence is within your reality once you give up the myth of magical money.

As you go through your day today, live in the real world, not in the smoke and mirrors of magical money.

Today's the day!

19

An Education
About College

I'm a huge believer and beneficiary of a higher education experience. My degrees in psychology and sociology benefit me every day, and many of the relationships I've enjoyed for over 40 years began in college including the one with my wife, Crystal. I have invested heavily through my foundation in higher education. At my alma mater, I funded the Stovall Administrative Center, the Stovall Center for Entrepreneurship, and a scholarship that has benefited hundreds of students.

In conjunction with my scholarship, each year I receive a number of applications from students seeking financial aid. The percentage of these students drowning in student loan debt is increasing dramatically. I am shocked and dismayed every time I read about an elementary education major or social work student who already has six-figures in debt with several semesters of college yet to go.

Whether you're dealing with your own tuition expenses or that of your children and grandchildren, you have to manage college expenses like any other area of your financial plan or the mounting costs and overwhelming debt will destroy your financial future and millionaire aspirations.

———

There is another financial crisis looming in our economy. It's not a credit card crisis or another mortgage meltdown. The devastating crisis on the horizon is the looming tsunami of student loan debt. Recent statistics reveal that 27% of Americans reach retirement age still owing on student loans.

Tim Maurer is one of the great minds in the personal finance field today. I have previously co-authored two books with Tim, *Financial Crossroads* and *The Ultimate Financial Plan*. Tim's new book, *Simple Money*, deals with a myriad of financial topics including how to fund a higher education while building a bright financial future.

I'm a firm believer in the value of a great education, but as Warren Buffett said, "People know the cost of everything and the value of nothing." With rare exceptions, when you look at college costs, higher prices do not always indicate greater value. In the vast research that was the basis for the bestselling book *The Millionaire Next Door*, it was revealed that a college diploma does have value in the marketplace and can be a good investment throughout a lifetime of work. However, higher tuition did not result in greater wealth.

Unless an individual is heading to law school, medical school, or a similar profession, it makes little difference where an individual receives their bachelor's degree. In many areas, there are no-cost or low-cost junior colleges or community colleges whose credits transfer directly into a state university. If you pursue this course within the state where you are a resident, you may discover that you can graduate with a four-year degree and have little or no student loan debt, particularly if you are willing to work during the summers and throughout the school year.

While some college students may feel that working while attending classes and studying may hurt their academic performance, statistics show that working up to 25 hours a week can actually result in a better grade point average. I believe that the discipline required to balance work and study can produce a better student.

Student loan debt is dangerous as it is very easy to acquire and very difficult to pay off. Young people who couldn't otherwise qualify to rent an inexpensive apartment or buy a used car can instantly obligate themselves to tens of thousands of dollars in student loan debt. In most cases, student loans, along with tax obligations, are among the only debts that cannot be discharged in a bankruptcy.

It's also important to remember that student loans remain whether you complete college and get a degree or

> The discipline required to balance work and study can produce a better student.

not. For these reasons, taking on student loan debt should be thought of like getting a tattoo. It may seem like a good idea at the time, but it will be with you into the future and can prove difficult, painful, and nearly impossible to get rid of.

As you go through your day today, learn the rules about getting a college education before you start.

Today's the day!

20

Living and Giving

Throughout the first half of my working life, I labored under the false impression that success was a matter of going from poverty to prosperity. Only when I became wealthy did I come to understand that I had only reached the midway point on the journey to success. True success only comes when we move from poverty through prosperity to purpose.

Throughout the 25 years I have written the *Winners' Wisdom* column read by people around the world, I've received countless questions and comments indicating that people believe that once they become wealthy, they will start giving. In reality, if you're not a giver today, you probably never will be.

Regardless of your financial condition, a portion of every dollar should be spent on your immediate needs, a portion should be invested for your future goals, and a portion should be given away.

This giving spirit not only applies to your money, but it also applies to your time. In fact, when you begin your financial

> **True success only comes when we move from poverty through prosperity to purpose.**

journey, you will be able to give away more of your time and less of your money. After you become a millionaire, you may have less time, but you will be able to give away much more money. The surest way I know to get what you want out of life is to be happy with what you have, and that begins with becoming a giver.

When I consult with corporate leaders, entrepreneurs, and success-minded people who read my books or these columns, attend one of my speeches, or watch one of my movies, they often tell me they are unhappy and dissatisfied in their personal and professional life. I am in the habit of then asking them, "Can you tell me about how you are currently giving your money and your time to others?" The standard response is, "What does that have to do with me being unhappy?" My simple answer is, "Everything."

Success is a follow-the-leader endeavor. We should never take advice from anyone who doesn't have what we want, and we should seek out those who do have what we want in order to emulate their behavior. Here's what a few people I respect and admire have to tell us about giving:

- "No one is useless in this world who lightens the burdens of another." Charles Dickens

- "We make a living by what we get. We make a life by what we give." Winston Churchill

- "You can give without loving, but you can never love without giving." Robert Louis Stevenson

- "For it is in giving that we receive." St. Francis of Assisi

- "One of the most important things you can do on this earth is to let people know they are not alone." Shannon L. Alder

- "When you give others a new chance, a new chance is really being given to you." Bryant McGill

- "You have not lived today until you have done something for someone who can never repay you." John Bunyan

- "To ease another's heartache is to forget one's own." Abraham Lincoln

In the aftermath of the disasters in Houston, Florida, and Puerto Rico, many of us were prompted to give of our time and money. While I certainly applaud and am pleased to participate in the current recovery efforts, giving of our time and money must be a consistent part of our lives. Hurricanes, earthquakes, and other overwhelming disasters get a lot of attention, but there are people all around us who are suffering every day who need a bit of our time, resources, and attention.

I lived far below the poverty level for several years when I was young and have also enjoyed living the last few decades as a multimillionaire. There are many elements of being wealthy that I appreciate, but the most fun and satisfaction I have ever gotten from my money is in the process of giving it away.

As a professional speaker, I enjoy commanding tens of thousands of dollars to make high-profile arena speeches; but for every such speech, I do one event for charity. Some of my most enjoyable appearances have been at nursing homes, school classrooms, and fundraising events for small charities trying to get started.

As you go through your day today, if you want to have more, do more, and be more, find a way to give more.

Today's the day!

To succeed, you've got to form good habits and start now.

21

The Tortoise and the Hare

Over the years of distributing the weekly *Winners' Wisdom* column in newspapers, magazines, and online publications around the world, financial questions are far and away the most prevalent inquiries we receive. Many of those questions involve get-rich-quick schemes that invariably never pan out.

Becoming a millionaire is a relatively slow and boring process for most people. Unless you're a world-class athlete, A-list movie star, or win the lottery, you likely won't become a millionaire quickly. Unfortunately for them, the rare people who do gain wealth rapidly often lose it rapidly. The process of slowly building wealth will give you the time and experience to learn how to manage it, keep it, and pass it on.

* * *

Any activity performed consistently over a long period of time can produce results. If you sit at a desk every day in a chair that has wheels or castors on it, you will travel, on average, eight miles each year while sitting at your desk. We all remember the famous story of the tortoise and the hare. While the hare is obviously faster, the tortoise wins the race based on consistency, not speed. We live in a microwave society, and unfortunately, oftentimes a crockpot effort is what success requires.

Psychologists tell us that any activity you perform for 21 days in a row will become a habit. A habit is nothing more than an activity that you engage in with little or no conscious thought. For most of us, our morning routine of getting ready to go to work or school is based on a series of habits. If someone asks them, otherwise intelligent people have to think about whether they brushed their teeth or not because they performed the task without even thinking about it. Great chefs often struggle to provide a set recipe when requested because so much of their process is done unconsciously as a habit.

> The process of slowly building wealth gives you time and experience to learn how to manage it, keep it, and pass it on.

I believe that our attitude is the most important element of success; however, our attitude does not directly impact our results. It instead impacts our actions which, over time, become habits that, in turn, do, indeed, impact our success.

I'm reminded of a story I call A Tale of Two Sisters. Anyone who regularly invests $10 a day in an average index fund can become wealthy over a normal working life. However, starting the habit early is a critical element because time is your ally in success.

Once upon a time, there were twin sisters who attended an investment seminar on their 18th birthday. The seminar leader encouraged everyone to start an investment plan for their retirement. Sister A got excited and began regularly investing while Sister B procrastinated, saying, "I've got decades before I retire." On their 30th birthday, Sister A revealed to Sister B the impressive amount she had amassed over the last 12 years. Sister B finally got inspired and invested consistently from age 30 until she retired at age 65. Sister A lost her momentum and never invested again beyond her 30th birthday. At age 65, Sister B had invested for over 35 years while Sister A had only invested for 12 years.

Both sisters had invested the same amount each month during the years they contributed to their retirement plans. Conventional wisdom would say that Sister B would have significantly more money; however, as often happens, conventional wisdom would be incorrect because Sister A was able to retire with significantly more money than her twin. Both sisters accumulated wealth by applying a habit regularly over a number of years, but Sister A added the secret sauce made up of getting started early.

As you go through your day today, realize that to succeed you've got to form good habits and start now.

Today's the day!

22

The Debt Trap

Recently, I participated in one of the largest surveys ever done regarding the habits and lifestyles of millionaires. Among other things, this survey showed that except for some business and tax strategies, millionaires avoid all debt. I can hear you saying what I would have said when I was in poverty if I had been confronted by that statement, "If I were a millionaire, I wouldn't be in debt either."

In reality, millionaires don't avoid debt because they're rich. They're rich because they avoid debt. The first step toward your millionaire destiny is to get out of the hole of debt you have created, and the first step to getting out of any hole is to stop digging.

———— ·——·——·——· ————

I own and operate a television network, do regular segments on national and local radio, and write these columns each week that appear in newspapers, magazines, and online publications

> **Millionaires don't avoid debt because they're rich. They're rich because they avoid debt.**

around the world. The one thing that all these media outlets have in common is that they live or die based on advertising. In the past several years, one of the fastest-growing types of advertising is debt. Whether it's credit card offers, car loans, or debt-relief programs, it's hard to go more than a few minutes without being confronted with an ad about debt. It seems to invade every part of our lives.

In the last 50 years, debt has gone from being a luxury for a few, to a convenience for many, to an addiction for most, and now a disease for all. Many people here in the United States, including me, are worried about our overwhelming national debt. It is a symptom of the crisis that is touching every area of society. Our government is made up of *We, the People*, and the debt that has been accumulated by our elected officials is a result of our willingness to accept high levels of debt in our personal lives.

Ironically, in the midst of this ocean of debt, there are a growing number of individuals who are choosing to live their lives debt-free. As hard as it is for many people to believe, approximately one-third of personal residences in America have no mortgages. Many of the cars you see on the road today were paid for with cash, and there are many families who send their kids to college without the burden of student loan debt.

I believe in living debt-free but continuing to make house, car, and college payments; but instead of making them to banks or finance companies, I believe these payments should be made to yourself. If after you pay off your home mortgage, you continue making a monthly payment that you channel into investments, you will likely retire early as a millionaire. If you pay off your car but continue to make similar payments into your own car account, within a few short years, you will be able to walk onto any car lot and pay cash for your next automobile. If you will approach college expenses and retirement as a long-term project involving regular monthly payments to yourself, you will find that facing the prospect of your children or grandchildren going to college along with the idea of your own retirement to be things you no longer dread but goals you're looking forward to.

As you go through your day today, commit to breaking the bonds of slavery and live your life debt-free.

Today's the day!

23

A Financial Emergency

This column was written in the aftermath of the 2008 financial crisis. The conditions we call depressions, recessions, or downturns are not really a financial crisis as much as they are cyclical conditions. Warren Buffett said, "You can't tell who's swimming naked until the tide goes out."

I remember when we had a leak in our roof at the Narrative Television Network office building. A maintenance engineer who no longer works here told me, "The roof only leaks when it's raining." While there's some obvious truth in that statement, you can't live that way or even keep a job as a maintenance person. A rainstorm is not a crisis, it's a weather condition that happens regularly.

I own property that is slightly above the 100-year flood plain. Water has never risen to a level where it impacted that property in recorded history. I'm willing to risk a 100-year flood, but I'm not willing to suffer through regular rain showers.

That which most people identify as a financial crisis, is nothing more than a regular occurrence for which they were not prepared.

———

We have all heard and read a lot recently about the financial crisis or monetary emergency that we are facing. These reports, most often, define the looming disaster in terms of billions or even trillions of dollars. While we are certainly facing some difficult economic times around the world, the most critical financial emergency we are facing, individually and collectively, is represented by $1,000.

A recent survey showed the staggering reality that 64% of Americans don't have $1,000 set aside as an emergency fund. This is an alarming statistic because, with the cost of all the complex devices that make our world possible, a non-functioning refrigerator, broken transmission, or even a leaky roof can use up a $1,000 emergency fund and more. It's not a matter of *if* you're going to have a thousand-dollar emergency. It's a matter of *when*.

These 64% of respondents to the survey were asked what they would do if they had an emergency since they don't even have $1,000 set aside:

- 9% said they would take out a loan;

- 17% declared they would borrow from friends or family;

- 9% replied they would get a cash advance on a credit card;

- 17% replied they would simply disregard other monthly expenses to cover the cost of the emergency; and

- 12% actually said they would have to sell or pawn some of their personal possessions.

In my latest book, *The Ultimate Financial Plan,* my co-author Tim Maurer and I explore every aspect of the financial decisions that are faced by you and your family; but it all starts with an emergency fund.

There is a tremendous benefit to having an emergency fund that goes far beyond covering the cost of an emergency. It could commonly be defined as a good night's sleep. If you are one of the majority of Americans who don't have even a minimal $1,000 emergency fund, you need to declare your own emergency now, and begin compiling reserve funds for that next inevitable bump in the road. You can turn a broken air conditioner, a visit to the minor emergency medical center, or an unanticipated tax bill into an annoyance instead of living with these realities as a looming emergency.

The number-one cause of divorce, depression, and dissatisfaction in our society is reported to be worry over money matters. I have to believe that the majority of the worry is not about retirement, college education, or paying off the house. Most worries are about those routine, daily matters that come to us unexpectedly and can only be resolved with money. Money is far from the most important thing in life; however, with respect to the problems that money solves, there is simply no substitute.

> Declare your emergency now, and begin compiling reserve funds for that next inevitable bump in the road.

As you go through your day today, realize that relaxation and peace of mind may be only $1,000 away.

Today's the day!

24

Wisdom Equals Wealth

It has been said that King Solomon was both the wisest and richest man of his era. If you're ever given a choice between wisdom and money, choose wisdom and you will have both. A lot of people can get money short term, but if they are going to live with wealth and maintain a millionaire lifestyle, they will have to apply wisdom.

Most people who live in the industrialized world earn more than enough money to become a millionaire. Too often though, for every dollar they get, they spend a dollar and a half. One way to never become wealthy is to try to borrow money so that you can look like you're already a millionaire.

I grew up in Oklahoma where I make my home today. In ranch country, someone who tries to look wealthy is labeled "all hat and no cattle." They may look like someone in a movie who owns a ranch with thousands of head of cattle, but in reality, they can't afford a hamburger.

If you were to ask any segment of our population what they believed it would take for them to be wealthy, the vast majority would give the simple answer, "Money." Making, earning, or being given more money does not make you wealthy. Wealth is the accumulation of money. I have encountered many people through my work in the area of financial education who make over $1 million in income and have little or no net worth. Some of these million-dollar earners actually have a negative net worth.

> **If given a choice between wisdom and money, choose wisdom and you will have both.**

Building wealth, at some point, becomes a matter of spending less than you earn. Recent financial studies in the professional sports industry reveal that by the time they have been retired for two years, 78% of former NFL players have gone bankrupt or are under financial stress, and 60% of former NBA players have gone broke within five years of retirement.

Most sports fans and observers of professional athletes mistakenly assume that professional football players or basketball players have it made financially. They assume these ball players are instantly made wealthy for the rest of their lives. Once again, we have to remember that wealth is a process of spending less than you bring in, and accumulating money so that your money can earn more money. This compounding is what creates permanent wealth and passive income.

If you make $1 million a year and spend $2 million a year, or like some of the athletes cited who make $10 million a year and spend $15 million a year, you are not as wealthy as someone who earns a modest income but habitually saves and invests 15% or 20% of their monthly cash flow. Wealth is not a function of what you earn. It's a function of what you do with what you earn.

If you don't understand these principles, like many pro athletes, a high income will only serve as a counterproductive financial tool to leverage you into more debt and obligations. If we took all the money in the world and divided it up equally among the population, within a few short years, those who are wealthy today would be wealthy again, and those who are in debt today would find themselves in financial distress once again.

Income is not the key to wealth. Knowledge is the key to wealth. But that knowledge will only generate permanent net worth for you when it is applied in the form of wisdom. Most people realize that they have to save and invest to accumulate wealth; however, for a myriad of reasons, they don't do it. We don't fail because we don't know what to do. We fail because we don't do what we know. Someone who knows and understands a financial principle but fails to apply it is no better off than someone who remains ignorant of the financial formula or concept in the first place.

As you go through your day today, commit to learning, understanding, and applying the financial concepts that will turn your income into wealth.

Today's the day!

25

Do You Feel Lucky?

A gun, an automobile, or money are all tools that can help us perform useful tasks and make our lives better. But none of them can help us, and they will likely hurt us, if we don't know how to handle them.

In my work with billionaire families in the aftermath of *The Ultimate Gift* movie trilogy based on my novels, I remind the mega-rich that passing along their valuables without sharing their values is a form of intergenerational child abuse. The same lessons you will need to learn to build wealth will reveal the knowledge you need to keep and maintain wealth.

I've been privileged to have a ringside seat to observe those who have instantly obtained huge amounts of money. Unless they get training and wise people around them, they will be like the child who was given a new gun or an automobile for their fifth birthday. Money is neither good nor bad. It is a tool. Whether it helps us or harms us will be determined by the knowledge and wisdom we apply to it.

I'm always embarrassed to tell my audiences at arena events, listeners to my radio shows, or readers of this column that when I could read with my eyes like you are reading these words in a newspaper, magazine, or online publication somewhere in the world, I don't know that I ever read a whole book cover to cover.

After losing my eyesight, I was part of a high-speed digital audiobook study sponsored by our government. When the study was concluded, I continued high-speed listening, and today, on average, I read one book a day. Becoming a reader made me want to be a writer, and of my 50 books, approximately 20 of them are novels, and nine have been made into movies.

I remain convinced that motion pictures are one of the most powerful communication mediums ever devised. I have often said if Mark Twain, the Apostle Paul, or William Shakespeare were alive today, in addition to writing books, they would be making movies.

> Passing along valuables without sharing values is a form of intergenerational child abuse.

I have stood in arenas full of thousands of people and quoted half of a famous line from a movie that is over 50 years old. Invariably, audiences will recite the remainder of the line in unison. One such line comes from Clint Eastwood's iconic character,

Dirty Harry. His simple statement, "Go ahead, make my day" is indelibly etched into our culture. Another of Dirty Harry's powerful lines is the question, "Do you feel lucky?" We tend to discount the power and reality of luck in our daily lives.

I got to participate in what became the largest survey of self-made millionaires ever done. When asked about the factors that resulted in financial success, the vast majority of those surveyed, including me, cited luck as a contributing element to becoming a millionaire. Luck comes to all of us. It's a matter of what we do with the good fortune we've been given.

One of the regular readers of this weekly column is a gentleman who is one of the largest single winners of the Powerball Lottery. After paying his taxes, he was left with several hundred million dollars. This windfall would represent a stroke of luck by any standard. However, if you look at the reality that plays out in the lives of those who have been lucky enough to win the lottery over the ensuing decade, on average, they suffer higher rates of divorce, bankruptcy, and suicide than the general population. Luck without preparedness, principles, and persistence can actually be counterproductive or even dangerous.

As you go through your day today, take advantage of luck and don't let it take advantage of you.

Today's the day!

26

From Wealth to Legacy to Dynasty

As you read these millionaire columns that have been compiled for this book from hundreds of *Winners' Wisdom* offerings written throughout a quarter of a century, you will notice that many of the ideas are repeated and restated in different and unique ways. It is important to reinforce the millionaire mentality and mindset because it does not come naturally, and the vast majority of people in our society you will encounter on a daily basis believe in myths and act in ways that will keep them in poverty.

Remember, poverty could be defined as one dollar less than it takes to provide all the things you want and need for you and your family. Wealth, on the other hand, is nothing more than the resources it takes to reach all of your personal and professional goals.

If you're going to act and live like everyone else, you don't have to learn or do anything unique. But if you're going to live the millionaire lifestyle, you will need to internalize principles and make them habits as you put them into daily practice. If you're going to have things that other people don't have, you're going to have to do things other people won't do.

———————

If you learn something, you can change your life. If you teach someone else what you have learned, you can change their life. But if you teach someone to teach, you can change the world.

Accumulating and maintaining wealth is not a matter of money. It, instead, is a matter of knowledge. If you divide all the money in the free world up evenly, within a few short years in our capitalistic system, the money will find its way back to where it is today. If you want to earn and accumulate wealth, find ways to create value in the lives of others. If you want to maintain wealth, seek knowledge and pass it on.

My late, great friend and mentor Coach John Wooden, rewrote the college basketball record books and set new standards that may never be equaled. I had the privilege of getting to know Coach Wooden and collaborate with him on a book during the last few years of his life. He passed away just before his 100th birthday, and his mind and spirit were sharp and intense to the end. He explained that getting ahead in a basketball game and staying ahead long enough to win the game are often two separate things. Teams that can outscore their opponent often get 10 or 12 points ahead and then try to play conservatively in order to hold their lead. Unfortunately, the skills it takes to get ahead

> To live the millionaire lifestyle, internalize principles, make them habits, and put them into daily practice.

and the skills required to stay ahead are quite different.

Dealing with wealth and money involves many of these same principles. Many hard-driving, creative entrepreneurs can generate wealth, but they are unable to maintain it and pass it on because they never master the concept of managing wealth.

In the aftermath of my book and the subsequent movie titled *The Ultimate Gift*, which dealt with generational wealth and wisdom transfer, I was asked by many billionaire and multi-millionaire families to speak at their family reunions and teach their second and third generations about money, success, and significance. Some of these families have only come into wealth in the current generation while others have experienced multiple generations of wealth and values transfer.

The families that can accumulate wealth and leave it to their heirs have created a legacy; but unfortunately, passing along your valuables without including your values, often results in disaster. On the other hand, the wealthy families who are able to pass along their money and attach it to principles in the form of lessons that can be shared for generations to come, create a dynasty. I believe every family, regardless of wealth, should pass along their history, lore, and perspective; but when there's extreme wealth involved, it should be passed along with extreme care and caution.

Your children, grandchildren, and their heirs should know and be able to pass on:

1. Where our family came from, how they lived, and how their lives affected later generations of the family.

2. Where did the family's wealth come from, and how was it created?

3. The next generation should know what their ancestors did before they were wealthy. If they worked for $1.00 a day doing manual labor and built an empire, it is great for future generations to know about and even experience that kind of manual labor.

4. Before wealth is handed over, there must be many lessons and a trial period much like you study to pass the driver's license exam and then practice using a learner's permit in the presence of an experienced driver until you can prove you are proficient.

5. Younger generations should be taught how and when they should share the family legacy with their children and how they keep the dynasty going and growing.

Money is the least valuable thing you will leave behind, but the lessons that have created money and maintained it are priceless.

As you go through your day today, remember to pass along your values along with your valuables.

Today's the day!

27

Diversions
and Disasters

My life ranges from ironic to absurd. I spend a great deal of my time writing books I can't read that are turned into movies I can't watch. When people discover I am blind, they often think that it's the worst fate that could befall anyone. For many years, a major psychological publication has done surveys of people's overwhelming fears. Losing one's eyesight is perpetually at or near the top of the list. Regardless of those surveys and people's beliefs, I feel like I'm the luckiest guy in the world, and I don't know anyone I would trade places with.

We are all as big or as small as that one thing that can divert us from where we need to be. This is why I repeatedly tell aspiring millionaires that they have to build an emergency fund. Building wealth is like growing a giant oak tree from an acorn. If you don't protect and preserve it when it first begins to sprout and is a few inches tall, you will never have a mighty oak.

If your wealth-building millionaire strategy can be derailed by a minor mechanical problem, repair bill, or medical treatment, you are doomed to fail.

I have long believed that we are all only as big as the smallest thing that it takes to divert us from our goals and our destiny. We live in a complex, high-tech world that requires many tools and accessories we use on a daily basis. Whether it's our computer, our sophisticated automobile, or our multi-functioning cellphone, 21st-century humans become lost without these items that started out as luxuries but have rapidly become necessities. These items become obsolete at an alarming rate and need replacing or repairing at a moment's notice.

In the process of writing these weekly columns, I do quite a bit of research. Occasionally, I will run across some information and statistics that simply defy belief. Following are some current financial statistics that were gathered in the process of a survey done by the Harvard Business School. The results of this survey caused me to have to catch my breath, then double and even triple check before drafting this column.

- Over half of Americans cannot raise $2,000 within 30 days from all sources, including savings, emergency funds, credit, or even family and friends.

- Twenty-five percent of households earning from $100,000 to $150,000 could not come up with the same $2,000 within 30 days from all available sources, including their family and friends.

- Forty percent of Americans will never save the first dollar for their retirement.

- The average retirement fund in America has approximately $35,000 in it. This would only generate a little over $100 a month throughout a long retirement before it was completely exhausted.

- Twenty percent of American households have no savings at all.

- Approximately half of all Americans die with no assets and leave liabilities behind.

- The average American household debt is currently $118,000.

If you live in a home, drive a car, use a computer, or depend upon a cell phone, it's only a matter of time until you face a major repair or replacement bill. A visit to a doctor's office or a pharmacy for a relatively minor ailment or illness can cost hundreds or even thousands of dollars. These are not the tragedies or disasters that traditionally we buy insurance to protect us from. These are daily occurrences that are definitely headed in your direction.

I have the opportunity through my speaking engagements and special events to work with many billionaire and multi-millionaire families. They live wonderful lifestyles and create

> A fully funded emergency fund can take looming disasters and turn them into minor annoyances.

great opportunities for their families, loved ones, and causes that matter to them. No matter how much wealth you may accumulate, however, the most satisfying and rewarding asset you will ever have is not a mansion, a sports car, or expensive jewelry. It is, instead, a fully funded emergency fund. You can take the looming disasters that most Americans who comprise the statistics above are facing, and turn those disasters into minor annoyances simply by having an emergency fund available to you at all times.

Most financial experts agree that an emergency fund should have three to six months of your regular income. While I agree that this would be an optimal amount for an emergency fund, most Americans would benefit greatly from having just one month's expenses in an emergency savings account. If you can only save 8 percent of your income each week, you will reach this initial goal of having one month's income in a savings fund within a year.

The average American household income is a little over $40,000 annually. After taxes and regular withholdings, the take-home income for this average family is approximately $2,800 per month. If this average family would save only $50 per week, they would at least have a minimal emergency fund set aside within a year, and then every time the car makes a strange noise, the roof begins to drip, the computer screen goes blank, or worse, when a child begins to cough, their first thought would not involve an immediate financial panic.

To reach our goals in life, we have to have daily focus and intensity. This is impossible to do if every minor bump in the road looks like a mountain range.

As you go through your day today, create a financial buffer between you and modern-day minor financial distractions by creating an emergency fund.

Today's the day!

28

Driving Over the Cliff

Over the 25-plus years of writing the weekly *Winners'*
Wisdom columns, I have dealt repeatedly with the
potential pitfalls and hidden dangers of owning and
operating an automobile. You will find the topic in several of the
sections in this book because automobiles represent the largest
purchase the vast majority of people will ever make that goes
down in value.

Buying something that is declining in worth from the moment
you take possession of it is bad enough, but you can compound
the disastrous impact on your financial future when you borrow
money to make an automobile purchase. The following column
was written in 2018, and I can assure you the statistics are worse
today than they were then.

When my wife and I got married, we purchased a horrible
used car that cost $350. It didn't take us long to realize we had
paid way too much for that car we affectionately called The
Green Dog. While we were driving around in that automobile,

that many people found to be an object of derision and ridicule, we developed and committed to our millionaire strategy.

Among the other steps in our plan, we committed to get out of debt, create an emergency fund, and start an investment portfolio which we continue to manage to this day. Then our plan called for us to pay cash for our next car. We really wanted a four-door Mercedes sedan. Suffice it to say that the floor mats in a Mercedes sedan cost more than our Green Dog car was worth.

There have been several memorable milestone moments in our millionaire journeys. One of them was driving onto the Mercedes lot and paying cash for our second car. This was after the owner of the Mercedes dealership made us park The Green Dog in the alley behind their service garage.

Going from The Green Dog to the Mercedes sedan reminded me of Neil Armstrong's words. It was one small step, but it was also a giant leap.

We can create a crisis in our lives when we elevate certain purchases to the level of a status symbol. We need to judge ourselves based on our character, our achievements, and our legacy, not which items we buy. You are not your purchases. If we're going to create wealth, we must stop buying things we don't need, with money we don't have, to impress people who don't care.

According to the American Automobile Dealers Association, the average car payment in the United States today is $503 over

> To create wealth, we must stop buying things we don't need, with money we don't have, to impress people who don't care.

84 months. This is a staggering number when you realize people are borrowing tens of thousands of dollars to buy something that is going down in value.

A recent nationwide survey revealed that 6.3 million Americans are at least three months late on their car payments. This is a bad sign for our economy and a worse sign for the families involved in these horrible transactions.

If you were to take the same $503 a month and invest it throughout your working life in an average growth stock mutual fund or index fund, you would be a millionaire many times over.

The true cost of borrowing money to buy an automobile can't just be calculated in the cost of the car. You must add in depreciation and the value of the investments or opportunities you could have taken advantage of with the same monthly payment.

I'm a multimillionaire today but spent the first decade of my adult life in poverty. I understand that, for many families today, buying an automobile is a daunting task. However, most car dealers, mechanics, and industry experts will tell you that you can buy a vehicle that will provide very reliable and dependable transportation for somewhere around 8 to 10 thousand dollars.

I'm generally not in favor of anyone borrowing money to buy a car, but if that is your reality, try to follow these guidelines. Find a car that you can purchase with no more than three years of payments. Plan to drive that car for at least six years so that during the first three years, you make payments on the car loan, and then the next three years, you make payments to yourself. This creates an amount of cash equal to the value of your car so you can consider buying your next automobile without a loan. I realize this is not popular among average consumers, but I can assure you it is popular among self-made millionaires.

Will Rogers may have said it best almost a century ago. "America will go down in history as the only nation on earth that will go to the poorhouse in an automobile."

Cars are a tool to get us from one point to another. To the extent they do this reliably, dependably, and affordably, they are a valuable asset; but if you think a car is going to make people think you're wealthy, the joke's on you as the charade will keep you from accumulating true wealth and driving any car you want to in the future.

As you go through your day today, make your car a tool of your success, not a tool of your bank's success.

Today's the day!

29

Reasonable Discomfort

As you read the following column, I hope you will have several takeaways. First, please remember that my influence and relationship with you and your millionaire aspirations is not limited to this book. I hope you will be one of the growing number of people who will stay in touch with me with questions about your specific millionaire journey as well as to share your millionaire milestones along the way.

I also hope you will remember that whether it's gaining wealth or anything else you want in your life, the old adage is true that *you don't get something for nothing.* Becoming a millionaire or achieving any other goal in your life is invariably a matter of what you're willing to give up to get what you want. When we are shopping for cars, clothes, furniture, or anything else, if the item initially appears to be something we might like to have, we will inevitably look at the price. Only then can we determine if that item is worth what we have to give up to get it.

No matter how wealthy you become, you will need to remember that you can have anything you want, but you can't have everything. Becoming a millionaire is a matter of choice, and that one choice will open many other doors for you.

＊━━━━＊━━━━＊

After writing this weekly column, which appears in hundreds of publications around the world for more than 25 years, the question I am most often asked about *Winners' Wisdom* is, "Where do you get ideas for all the columns?" I have written over 1,000 columns which, to date, have filled four hardcover volumes published in conjunction with The Napoleon Hill Foundation entitled *Wisdom for Winners*. Readers of these columns would be surprised to learn that many of the ideas come from *Winners' Wisdom* readers. People often contact me, as I hope you will do, to ask questions or make comments (jim@jimstovall.com).

> Becoming a millionaire or achieving any life goal life is invariably a matter of what you're willing to give up to get what you want.

Recently, I received an email from a gentleman describing how he and his wife were experiencing "reasonable discomfort" as they build their business and strive for success. Although I've never heard it put in those terms, virtually all successful people would recognize the concept of reasonable discomfort as they have, invariably, lived with it for a period of time while they were creating success.

My late, great friend and colleague Zig Ziglar often said, "We don't pay the price for success. We enjoy it. But we pay the price for failure."

As I look back into my past from my current position of relative wealth and success, I remember times when my wife and I slept on the floor in the office because we couldn't afford an apartment and drove a decrepit automobile known as The Green Dog which has become world famous after being memorialized in several of my books. These struggles from the past—which at the time seemed daunting—are now actually humorous and provide context for enjoying success.

Success is often a function of being willing to do what other people are not willing to do, or in some cases, being willing to do without what other people won't do without in order to build success. My friend and colleague Dave Ramsey is undoubtedly responsible for helping to get more people out of debt than anyone throughout history. Dave often says, "You've got to be willing to live like no one else so someday you can live like no one else."

All of us live with a certain amount of deprivation as there are always things we would like to have, but if we're sacrificing for our own success instead of experiencing a degree of failure, "reasonable discomfort" becomes the price we are paying for success, not the result of our failure.

As you go through your day today, consider what you can sacrifice for your future success.

Today's the day!

30

Stock Market Perspective

As you will read in the following column, in my business career, I have seen the stock market grow 30-fold. To say I am bullish on the stock market in the long term would be an understatement. Please keep in mind you should never invest any funds in equities that you cannot leave there for at least five years. If you look at the track record of five-year periods in the stock market, there is very little risk. If you extend it to ten years or throughout your working life, the risk is diminished further.

The only way you can evaluate the element of risk in your investments, or any other area of life, is to determine what is the potential reward. If you buy a lottery ticket, the risk is immense as you will likely lose your money. Millions of people buy lottery tickets—I am not among them—but they obviously have determined that the potential reward offsets the risks they are taking.

People invariably buy into the smoke and mirrors presented by the financial channels and the news media about how government policy, regulations, and politics will impact their investments. I'm not as concerned about what happens in the White House or on Wall Street as much as I'm concerned about what happens in your house on your street.

The stock market is not a measure of how the economy is doing. It is a measure of how people *think* the economy is doing. Often that perception becomes reality.

I began my business career as a young college graduate running my own New York Stock Exchange firm office. I clearly remember the day in the 1980s I was sitting at my desk when the Dow Jones Industrial Average—the most recognized barometer of the market—went over 1,000 and stayed above that level. The stock market had existed for well over a century and had finally reached the 1,000-point milestone.

Today, as the market sits above 30,000, it seems that it passes 1,000-point milestones like a speeding car passes telephone poles along the side of the highway. This market will adjust at some point because it always has, and this market will go up again because it always does.

When you invest in the stock market, you are investing in free enterprise and capitalism. Recently, due to some convoluted media coverage, the stock market, politics, and the economy have been co-mingled and referred to interchangeably by some so-called experts. I realize there are many people reading these

> ## "Kid, the best time to invest in the stock market is when you've got some money."

words who are in favor of the current administration, and there are other readers who are not. I am more concerned that you are involved in the political process than I am concerned about which side you choose.

In recent days, I've had a number of people who are fully invested in the stock market—either on their own or through a retirement plan—tell me they are opposed to the current leadership in Washington. Politically, we all express our preferences and invest our political capital when we vote. Economically, we express our preferences and invest our financial capital when we move in and out of the stock market.

For most people around the world, the U.S. stock market remains the most reliable and dependable growth investment. While our economy certainly has challenges and our country needs to correct some financial policies, I would never recommend that anyone bet against the U.S. economy and free enterprise.

As a young man running that investment office, I remember asking one of the grizzled, old Wall Street veterans about the best time to invest in the market. Three decades later, I still remember his response. "Kid, the best time to invest in the stock market is when you've got some money."

The stock market will continue to move up and down, but it's a lot more fun to be speeding along the highway passing the thousand-point milestones than it is to be standing beside the road watching the parade pass you by.

As you go through your day today, work hard for your money, and make sure it works hard for you.

Today's the day!

Permanent wealth
has less to do
with money than
our attitude.

31

Being Happy for the Joneses

In the field of goals and achievements, which would certainly include becoming a millionaire, your attitude and world-view will inevitably impact your efforts which will, in turn, impact your results. Too many people mistakenly believe that an abundance mentality or millionaire mindset comes from having wealth. In reality, the wealth is a result of the mindset and your underlying attitudes regarding money. If you think money is evil or unattainable, your performance will reflect these beliefs and your results will follow.

We become like the people we spend the most time with. Since 98 percent of people have not and will not reach their financial goals, you have to proactively structure spending quality time with the people who have what you want. The fastest way to change your attitude about becoming a millionaire is to spend time with millionaires. You will rapidly discover they are ordinary people with extraordinary goals and beliefs.

The phrase "keeping up with the Joneses" has become synonymous with wanting things we don't have. Too often, this emotion involves acquiring things we don't need while spending money we don't have in order to impress people who don't care. In my own journey from poverty to prosperity and through the research involved in writing many of my books, I've come to the conclusion that permanent wealth has less to do with money than our attitude.

There are two basic world views relating to money. There is a scarcity mentality which assumes there's a finite amount of wealth so that if someone else succeeds, you inevitably fail; and then there is an abundance mentality involving the belief that there is more than enough for everyone to acquire all they need and want.

If there were a litmus test for your view of wealth, it would involve how you feel when others around you succeed. If you are happy for them and celebrate their success, you have an abundance mentality. On the other hand, if you are jealous or resent their success, you have a scarcity mentality.

I have long believed that if you took all the money in the world and divided it up evenly, within a few short years, those who are currently wealthy would be wealthy once again, and those who are failing financially would find themselves struggling again. This example precludes the many people around the world who do not have access to a free enterprise capitalistic society in which they can succeed or fail based on their own merits.

Acquiring wealth requires purpose and focus. Unless there's something you want to specifically do with money, there is no reason to have it. The only three items you can spend your money on are things, memories, and security. A portion of every dollar you have should be spent on your current needs, a portion should be saved and invested for your future needs, and a portion of every dollar should be given away.

> If all the money in the world was divided evenly, I believe that within a few short years, those currently wealthy would be wealthy again, and those failing financially would be struggling again.

Most people spend all they earn and a little bit more via consumer debt having little or no savings or investments for the future—and rarely, if ever, think about giving. Constant and habitual giving is another indicator of an abundance mentality. Only those who believe they either have or are in the process of acquiring abundance, can freely give to others. Before you change your spending budget, your investment plan, or your retirement vehicle, change your attitude regarding money. You can never out-earn, out-save, or out-invest a scarcity attitude.

If you believe you are destined to always struggle financially, you will create the circumstances to meet your expectations. On the other hand, if you envision yourself living a life of abundance and providing for people and causes that you care about, your thoughts will manifest themselves in your life.

As you go through your day today, examine your attitudes about money, and change your life.

Today's the day!

32

A Cup of Retirement

There are many milestones you will achieve and pass on your way to becoming a millionaire, but everyone who builds wealth will go through two major transitions. The first transition is when you get out of debt. In accounting terms, your balance sheet will go from red ink to black, which signifies you have a positive net worth.

As absurd as it seems, there are an alarming number of people who have worked hard for decades and have a negative net worth. If you are among those drowning in debt, resolve to undergo the first major transition and get out of debt. The second major transition in your journey to becoming a millionaire involves the day you quit working for money, and your money begins working for you. For many years, we have mistakenly thought this was at age 65, but there's really nothing magic about that number, and you can financially retire whenever your wealth will allow it.

I have long followed a group that is identified by the initials F.I.R.E. This stands for Financial Independence Retire Early.

Retirement simply means you get to choose what you do.

If you do a bit of internet research on them, you will find people committed to retiring in their fifties, forties, or even thirties. Please remember that retirement doesn't mean that you don't do anything. It simply means you get to choose what you do, and you get off of that mind-numbing endless treadmill of trading your time for someone else's money.

There are many factors in 21st-century life that we must plan for. We should have car insurance to cover us while we're on the road as well as homeowners or renters' insurance to cover our possessions at home. Everyone should have a will whether they are wealthy or not.

Many people who do not have significant assets believe there is no need for them to have a will. However, if you have children and die without a will, your state government is going to decide who raises your children. If you're incapacitated, the state government will decide who handles your money and healthcare needs. While each of these eventualities can be covered, and may or may not occur, all of us will eventually retire if we live long enough.

When most pensions, retirement plans, and Social Security were established here in America, the average retiree only lived a few months past age 65. Today, the average worker reaching retirement age can look forward to 18 years of life in retirement. This is an amazing change and a wonderful development as it offers people many years to enjoy the fruits of their labor. However, we must all be prepared.

To paraphrase one of my heroes, Charles Dickens, retirement will either be the best of times or the worst of times based upon our planning and persistence. Our parents and grandparents could depend on company retirement plans or pensions, but we are going to have to do it ourselves. If you plan ahead, you will have a much more luxurious retirement than any of your ancestors. But if you don't plan ahead, it can be devastating without the pension or corporate retirement plan safety net.

As I review the current statistics regarding retirement balances, it seems to be a tale of two scenarios including the best of times and the worst of times. Some Americans started saving early and have remained consistent. They have invested in prudent growth funds and can look forward to living as literal multi-millionaires in their golden years. On the other hand, many Americans have no savings and no retirement. Their golden years are sadly going to be made of fool's gold.

Fully one-third of Americans spend more money on coffee than they put into their retirement savings. These are not poor people but, instead, are people who have poorly managed their assets. It's easy to put it off to some unspecified time in the future, but all you need to do to receive an abrupt wake-up call is realize that, for most people, a 40-year work-life is what they can expect.

If you've been working 20 years, you should be halfway to your retirement goals. This should either make you feel satisfied and relaxed as you look at your retirement balance or should give you a wake-up call jolt like a very large cup of strong coffee.

As you go through your day today, realize that a little planning and preparation now will make a huge difference later.

Today's the day!

33

You're Covered

You will notice in my syndicated column and in this book, I repeatedly stress the importance and the myriad of benefits from having an emergency fund. I would give up many luxury items and millionaire experiences to have a sizeable emergency fund, and beyond that, what I call an opportunity fund.

While an emergency fund is an antidote to bad things happening in your life, an opportunity fund is your ticket to many great things in your future. You should never use your emergency fund for opportunities, but it is well worth accumulating more liquid cash for the wonderful possibilities coming your way.

My mentor who was a graduate of the third grade and who amassed $10 million during the Great Depression, would often describe unsuccessful people pretending to be millionaires as someone who, "If it costs fifty dollars to go around the world, he couldn't get out of town."

While I've not yet seen a chance to go around the world for $50, my wife and I have enjoyed amazing trips, wonderful private concerts, and dining experiences as well as having an opportunity to buy all manner of products and services at ridiculously low prices simply because we had cash on hand in our opportunity fund.

Realize that when you have an emergency fund you will be in the very slim minority of people because the vast majority of individuals are subject to the next regular incident in their life that will invariably create a looming disaster. These individuals or businesses are often forced to liquidate very valuable things simply because they don't have an emergency fund.

If you have an opportunity fund, you can actually help them out of their current predicament and take advantage of amazing opportunities at the same time. Lest you think you're kicking people while they're down, whenever I acquire something from someone who was forced to sell it because they didn't have cash on hand, I always give them my speech on the value of an emergency fund. This can create a win/win for all concerned.

———◆———

Recently, I listened to a nationwide call-in radio show that focused on personal finance and consumer issues. I noticed that a number of callers from across the country were very worried or frantic about looming expenses and repairs. They were hopeful that they would be covered by warranties or insurance.

Unfortunately, most of the callers were devastated to learn that the pending financial obligation would not be paid for by a manufacturer's warranty or an insurance company. Occasionally, the host would let one of the worried callers know that they were, indeed, covered. Those callers heaved a sigh of relief and expressed their gratitude to the radio show's host for the good news. The simple phrase, "You're covered," seemed to be the antidote for fear, depression, and worry.

I'm very pleased to be able to share with you, the readers of this *Winners' Wisdom* column, how you can obtain an insurance plan or warranty that can cover virtually all unanticipated expenses for the rest of your life. This magical financial vehicle is commonly known as an emergency fund. Nothing in your financial life will bring you and your family the peace and contentment that an emergency fund can afford you. There is no product or service you can buy that will bring you more joy and happiness than eliminating the majority of financial stress and worry from your life.

An emergency fund is simply an account that holds approximately six months' worth of your living expenses in reserve to cover any unanticipated costs. While you should still have insurance coverage to protect you from huge risks, the greatest number of expenses faced by most consumers could be covered with a six-month emergency fund.

As your fund builds, you must remind yourself and your family that a sale at the mall, a weekend getaway, or a new pair of shoes do not constitute emergencies. You will still need discipline in your monthly budget, but the next time the car stalls, the refrigerator makes a strange noise, or the roof begins leaking, it will seem more of an annoyance than a crisis.

> No product or service you buy can bring you more joy and happiness than eliminating the majority of financial stress and worry from your life.

I believe that your emergency fund should be a major priority in your financial life. Once you've eliminated all consumer debt, you should establish your emergency fund even before you commit to long-term investing. While long-term investing will make or break your retirement or financial future, keeping everyday emergencies from derailing your financial plan is vital. When you consider that a significant factor in divorce, depression, and the growing rate of suicides is financial stress, you really can't overstate the importance of having an emergency fund.

As you go through your day today, commit to having an emergency fund and relax because you're covered.

Today's the day!

34

Consistently Consistent

As I was preparing to launch my millionaire journey while I was drowning in debt and had a negative net worth, I came across a little book that changed my views on money and everything else. *The Automatic Millionaire* is a quick read, and it quite simply tells you how to put your wealth-building efforts on autopilot.

I don't often express my appreciation for the IRS, but early in the last century, the Internal Revenue Service came to the understanding that if they were going to collect large portions of people's incomes in the form of taxes, they were going to have to take a little bit out of each check or they would never collect because by the time the tax deadline day rolled around, the money would be long gone.

We can all take a lesson from our Uncle Sam and pay ourselves the same way we pay our taxes. If you will simply put your retirement funds and regular deposits into your investment portfolio on automatic withdrawal, you will never see the money. It will be less painful because out of sight means out of mind and you will only have to make a decision and establish a commitment once.

Wealth is built with small amounts over an extended period of time. You can either depend on yourself to make thousands of good decisions or you can do it once and let the eighth wonder of the world, compounding interest, take over for you.

———◆———

Whether you're trying to accomplish something great or small in either your personal or professional life, you will find that there is no more important element of success than consistency. Achievement does not come from an instant emotional inspiration nor from an exhausting overwhelming expenditure of energy in the moment. Success comes from choosing a path and following it consistently regardless of feelings, emotions, conditions, or circumstances.

I venture out to a grocery store about once a decade, so the experiences are memorable. I remember on one of my infrequent visits, as I was standing in the checkout line, there seemed to be two schools of thought regarding how to pay for groceries and exit the store quickly. One group of people simply observed what they believed to be the shortest or fastest-moving line and stayed there until they completed the process.

The other group of people waited in one line until they thought another one was moving faster, then they rushed to get in the back of that line until they switched to yet another line.

As in the story of the tortoise and the hare, the people who chose a line and stayed in it seemed to find more success than those who frantically moved from line to line trying to find some sort of non-existent shortcut.

> **Wealth is built with small amounts over an extended period of time.**

Each weekend, emergency rooms and urgent care facilities fill up with people who get a sudden inspiration to play rugby, rock climb, or run marathons regardless of the fact that they have not been involved in any physical activity since high school. On the other hand, if you read stories of those who completed the Boston or New York City marathons, you will learn about people who were inactive for years but formed an exercise plan, often beginning with walking in their neighborhoods, followed by moderate jogging, and, eventually, conquering the 26-mile race.

Wealth is rarely generated from a single speculative stock pick. Instead, it usually comes from consistently investing in the broad market. The fastest growing group of millionaires are those who persistently and consistently invest in their 401K or other retirement vehicles, each month.

Whether you're exercising, investing, writing a book, or building a business, set your goal and formulate a realistic plan that involves a level of activity you can accomplish every day.

As you go through your day today, establish a daily routine you can live with, then get started.

Today's the day!

35

Taking Stock

One of the great challenges in writing a weekly syn-dicated column read by people in newspapers, magazines, and online publications around the world is that there is not much advice that is good for all people all the time. If you've ever heard a doctor on a call-in advice show on the radio, you will remember that the information they present has to be extremely generic because everyone listening to them has different symptoms and conditions. This book is designed to give you the mindset, motivation, attitudes, consistency, and framework to begin your millionaire journey. If and when you need more specific detailed advice, you can reach me at jim@ jimstovall.com.

In my life, I have professionals who oversee my health, my automobile, my appliances, my yard, and every area that deals with my day-to-day existence. Therefore, I want to have a dream team of advisors including a lawyer, a CPA, an investment adviser, insurance professional, and an estate planner to manage my wealth. As your money grows, your relationships with these professionals will increase accordingly. To the greatest extent possible, you and your dream team will need to make decisions before the fact, not after. This will help take the emotion out of trading various investments.

If you've already decided that when a certain stock rises to a particular level, you will liquidate some or all of it, you won't be tempted to hang on too long or bail out too soon.

As a young man, my greatest ambition was to be a professional football player. During a routine physical to go play another season, I was diagnosed with the condition that caused my blindness. I was fortunate to be able to pivot and complete my athletic career as an Olympic weightlifter, but I remain a huge fan of football.

A coach I greatly admire formulated a game plan that brought him and his team many victories and can help you and me achieve and maintain our millionaire goals. On the first play of the game, he would have his quarterback hand off to the running back who ran between the guard and tackle in what is known as a dive play. This is one of the simplest and safest plays in football. If the play resulted in a four-yard gain or more, he would run it again. When his critics in the media asked how long he would keep running that dive play, his simple response applies to football games or financial plans: "I'm going to keep doing what works until it doesn't work."

I began my entrepreneurial business career by opening my own office with a New York Stock Exchange member firm. As a young man, I helped my clients invest in stocks, bonds, commodities,

> "I'm going to keep doing what works until it doesn't work."

mutual funds, and every other publicly traded investment vehicle. Many of my clients were approaching or beyond retirement age and were very cautious about buying stocks because they or their parents had lived through the stock market crash and the Great Depression.

I understand that investing in common stock can be frightening and volatile, but if you are diversified and disciplined, it remains among the best investments available. When people ask why I invest in stocks, I explain that the year I was born, the Dow Jones Industrial Average, which is an index of the 30 largest stocks on the exchange, was trading at 439. At this writing, it is over 33,000.

This index, or the average of the stock market, has grown 75-fold in my lifetime. Please understand this return does not represent stocks that have done well or outperformed the market. It is simply an average return throughout those years. I don't know of any other investment that can consistently match this performance.

If you would like to calculate the market return from the year of your birth, your high school graduation, or any other year in the past, just go to https://www.fedprimerate.com/dow-jones-industrial-average-history-djia.htm.

As in most things, there's no simple investment answer, and a broad approach is best. A portfolio combining stocks and bonds, as well as other investment vehicles, is often preferable to just investing in the stock market. Still, it's hard to imagine a winning investment strategy that doesn't involve some exposure to the stock market.

This action plan is even valid if you are in your retirement years. During our grandparents' generation, many people did not live past the traditional retirement age of 65. Today, a 65-year-old needs to plan for another 30 years of life or more. The fastest-growing demographic in our country is made up of people over 100.

Your finances represent one of the most important areas of your life, as it can affect all the other aspects of your future. It certainly warrants you and me to establish an ongoing relationship with high-quality financial advisors.

As you go through your day today, take stock of your future.

Today's the day!

36

Price and Priority

I f we want to change any element of our lives, it begins with a thought, then a fully developed idea, and it finally becomes a goal with a specific plan attached. The great writer Napoleon Hill may have said it best, "Anything the mind can conceive and believe, it can achieve."

As a blind person myself, I've come to learn the difference between sight and vision. I had my eyesight for the first portion of my life, and now I've spent several decades as a blind person. While I would be the first to admit sight is a convenient thing to have, it pales in comparison to the value of having vision. You've heard people who questioned or doubted something say, "I'll believe it when I see it."

When it comes to you becoming a millionaire, the reality is, you'll see it when you believe it. It all begins with that initial vision of a different kind of life followed by a proactive plan to get from here to there.

During the financial struggles of my college career and the early years of my marriage, I remember sitting around with other people dealing with similar financial challenges and discussing what we would do if money were no object. The thoughts of expensive sports cars, wonderful homes, and first-class travel made our money troubles seem even more acute. Then, when I got on my wealth-building financial plan and became a millionaire, thoughts of luxury items and world-class experiences became a reality.

> **When it comes to you becoming a millionaire, the reality is, you'll see it when you believe it.**

I found that people living in relative poverty believe that wealthy individuals are totally focused on money to the exclusion of everything else. In reality, I discovered that when I didn't have money, it was a factor in every decision I made. After becoming financially independent, I realized that I rarely think about money at all. To people struggling with finances, the cost of anything is generally the first and foremost factor to be considered, and if they can't get past that financial hurdle, they generally dismiss the thought of the purchase or expenditure.

On the other hand, people of wealth tend to focus on value as opposed to price. They look at the potential pleasure an expenditure will bring or the good it will do in the world for other people. My mentor, Lee Braxton, had a third-grade education and became a self-made multimillionaire in the midst of the Great Depression. He often explained to me how financial attitudes could be best demonstrated in the way people read a restaurant menu. He explained that wealthy people go down the left side of the page and decide what they want to eat based on their preferences or nutritional plan. People with financial struggles look down the right side of the menu at the prices, and once they find a number they can afford, they look to the left and place their order.

As a writer, I've always admired the characters created by Charles Dickens. Ebenezer Scrooge is the template for greed and miserly behavior for generations of writers and readers. In the midst of Dickens' tale *A Christmas Carol*, Scrooge goes through a total shift of mindset and attitude with respect to money. He was the worst example of how to handle money in the beginning of the story, then he became a model of how we should all think about wealth at the end of the story.

Wealth, financial independence, and becoming a millionaire are much more about your mindset and your attitudes as opposed to dollars and cents. We should never gravitate toward anything simply because we can afford it. Instead, we should determine what is good, valuable, and can create the most positive impact, then figure out how to pay for it.

As you go through your day today, focus on priorities, not price.

Today's the day!

37

The Number

M any financial pundits and naysayers want to grab the spotlight and capture the headlines with gloom and doom predictions based on factors and events they claim to be totally unique. With confidence in their voice, they would like to assure us that we've never been here before and we've never even seen anything like this. My late, great friend and mentor Paul Harvey, who spent more than half a century bringing us the news and putting it into context, often repeated, "It's times like this that remind us there have always been times like this."

The value in studying history is not simply to become aware of events in the distant past, but instead to understand the trends because history does, indeed, repeat itself. Those who do not learn from history will suffer the consequences just as their ancestors did, but those who learn from history can benefit and prosper.

For those of you who are regular readers of these weekly columns or have read some of my more than 50 books, you know that I began my business career as an investment broker with a New York Stock Exchange member firm. As an investment broker, I helped

> "It's times like this that remind us there have always been times like this."

my clients reach their financial goals by navigating through the complex and mysterious maze of stocks, bonds, options, and all manner of investments.

I remember sitting in my office forty years ago, monitoring the direction and strength of the stock market. At that time, most brokers followed the market through the Dow Jones Industrial Average Index, which is a blended, weighted average of thirty large blue-chip stocks publicly traded on the exchange. This index is still used today by many brokers, along with other measurements that have been developed to monitor the market.

At that time, the Dow Jones Average was hovering around 1,000. It seemed to be fairly consistent in a trading range around that level. I remember attending a talk by a renowned financial expert and author on the long-range future of investing in business and industry through the stock market at that time. I will never forget when he said many of us in the room would live long enough to experience the Dow Jones Industrial Average reaching 30,000. The room was filled with other brokers and investment analysts, and everyone sat in stunned silence. The thought of that rock-solid index trading at a level thirty times its current value seemed to be total fantasy. As I dictate this column, the Dow Jones Industrial Average has eclipsed the 30,000 level and is now hovering at 40,000.

Sometimes the best way to understand where you are is to consider where you've been. As ludicrous as it may seem, I believe there are readers of today's column in newspapers, magazines, and online publications around the world who will live to see the major stock market indexes at a level equal to thirty or forty times their present value.

In 1903, Orville and Wilbur Wright changed history by flying their plane a little over a hundred feet. On that day, if you had told the brothers that, within their lifetime, airplanes would regularly cross the ocean and the era of jet travel would be well underway, they would have thought you were insane.

In the short term, the stock market can be very volatile and unpredictable; but in the long term, it can be reliable, dependable, and the key to financial independence for you and your family.

As you go through your day today, understand the past and present, and then chart your course into the future.

Today's the day!

38

Invest Like a Billionaire

If you were aware of my work at all before reading this book, it's probably because of a novel I wrote entitled *The Ultimate Gift*, the sequel books that followed, and the movie trilogy it inspired. In *The Ultimate Gift*, a billionaire, late in his life, realizes that lavishing his wealth on his family without instilling values in their lives had ruined many of them and created generations of greedy, petty people. He believes his grandson has potential to overcome the intergenerational trend, so instead of making him an instant millionaire through his will, the grandfather determines to send the young man on a yearlong odyssey involving twelve monthly lessons he calls gifts. Throughout the story, the young man learns the gift of work, family, friends, problems, laughter, and the gift of a day among others.

Originally, I was going to write the story based on lessons I learned from my own grandparents and parents. The lessons would have been the same but without the wealth that the character in the book and movie possessed. My idea in making the patriarch a billionaire was simply to dispel what I call the big lie.

When you reject the big lie, a life of significance and financial independence awaits.

The big lie that most people believe tells us that there are two kinds of people in the world. There are healthy, wealthy, successful people who get everything they want out of life. Then there are people like you and me who struggle and have to settle for mediocrity or even poverty. If you believe the big lie, it will become a self-fulfilling prophecy and will manifest itself in your life. If you reject the big lie, a life of significance and financial independence awaits.

* * *

You may have heard the old saying, "You have to have money to make money." In my adult life, I've been very poor and very wealthy. While it's certainly easier to make money when you have money, it's important to note that approximately 90% of millionaires are first-generation. These are people who started with little or nothing and accumulated wealth during their working lives. In reality, it's easier for people starting with nothing to build and manage wealth than ever before.

I routinely consult with a number of families of extreme wealth. I mostly advise them on the impact of wealth on their second and third generations. Most of these extended families have what is known in financial circles as a family office. It generally includes lawyers, accountants, estate planners, and investment experts who dedicate all of their time and professional expertise to working for one family.

While none of us have these types of resources when we begin our financial journey, here in the 21st century, we have access to many tools that our parents and grandparents could not have imagined.

I began my professional career as an investment broker for a New York Stock Exchange member firm. At that time, approximately 40 years ago, the only people who could get immediate quotes on stocks, bonds, and other investments were brokers like me or multi-millionaires. Everyone else had to get their stock quotations and portfolio valuations through the morning newspaper.

Thus, everyone was trying to make today's investment decisions based on yesterday's information. Driving while looking in the rearview mirror can be very difficult and dangerous. Today, you can get quotes up to the second for virtually every financial instrument issued anywhere in the world at the touch of a button on a device that is likely a few feet from where you are at this moment.

Research in previous generations was a tool that was exclusive to investors of extreme wealth. Today, you and I can review timely investment research from some of the greatest analysts in the field at any time. At the beginning of the last century, if people wanted to diversify across various investment sectors or the entire market, it took significant amounts of money and dedicated investment professionals. You and I can invest in mutual or index funds to meet our goals or objectives. We have all the billionaire tools available to us right now. But like any other tools, they are only effective if we use them.

As you go through your day today, start right where you are and invest like a billionaire.

Today's the day!

39

Cash Is Still King

Among the many benefits I have been blessed to enjoy as a result of becoming a millionaire is the periodic opportunity to travel on a private jet. One of my wealthy friends describes a private plane as a time machine because it eliminates all the wasted hours checking in at the airport, dealing with luggage, making connections, and all of the hassles of airline transportation.

One of the things I enjoy about being on a private jet is getting to talk with the pilots. I realized that altitude for a jet is much like cash for an individual or business. A routine challenge at 30,000 feet may be as simple as pushing a button or recalibrating a gauge. But if it happens at 1,000 feet, it can become a crisis that has to be dealt with instantly or disaster awaits.

Cash on hand will insulate you or your business from difficulties or disaster. Cash can buy you extra time, more resources, or the expertise needed to overcome any situation. If you're going to become a millionaire, you need to stop thinking about the cost

> Cash keeps the world of possibilities open for you. The scriptures remind us, "The borrower is slave to the lender."

of anything in terms of the monthly payments. A new car doesn't cost $586 per month. It costs $68,000. Debts and monthly obligations greatly increase your risk of disaster and limit your options. Cash keeps the world of possibilities open for you. The scriptures remind us, "The borrower is slave to the lender."

All of us who are in business should play to win. We keep score using money. While I would be the first to say that significance, service, values, and making a difference for others should be a primary goal in our work, each of these areas benefits from more resources.

Money doesn't equal good. It does equal more. If it is your goal to do good things and make a difference in the world, money will help you do better things and make a bigger difference. The value of any organization can be calculated in numerous ways and is often a matter of debate, but cash is universal. Everyone on the planet knows what a dollar is worth.

Recently, I heard that the Apple Corporation has more cash on hand than the United States government. This made me feel good about the money I have invested in Apple and not so good about the money that I have invested via taxes in the United States government. Companies and people who generate and keep cash have the most value.

Recently, there was a study done revealing the overall growth and return on various classes of stock since 1927. It was revealed that if you had invested $1,000 in the stock of companies that did not pay dividends, which are generally considered growth stocks, over the ensuing 80 years, your $1,000 would have grown to in excess of $800,000. This is a tremendous return, but the study went on to reveal that the same $1,000 investment in 1927 among the one-third of publicly traded companies that paid the lowest dividends would have grown to $1.3 million. The same investment in companies that ranked among the middle one-third of dividends paid to shareholders would have turned into $4 million; and before you invest your money, you need to know that $1,000 invested among companies that ranked in the upper one-third of dividends paid would have grown to $7.9 million.

Conventional wisdom would tell us that investing in startup companies that don't pay any dividends will yield the highest results when, in reality, investing in companies that are already successful and have enough cash on hand to pay out dividends to investors will yield ten times more investment return.

Before you invest, it's great to study charts, graphs, trends, and industry analyses, but before you put down your hard-earned dollars, take a hint from Jerry McGuire and ask someone to "Show me the money."

As you go through your day today, observe potential, examine trends, but count the cash.

Today's the day!

40

Automatic Millionaire

As you have already read in these pages, I am a fan of the little book *The Automatic Millionaire* and the concept it outlines. The most efficient, quickest, and easiest way to accomplish anything is to make the tasks involved a regular habit.

At this writing, nine of my more than 50 books have been turned into movies. When the producers of the first film saw me on stage at an arena event in Las Vegas, they got excited about the idea of having me play a cameo role in the movie. Initially, I rejected the idea thinking I didn't want to ruin the project with my non-existent acting skills.

Eventually they prevailed, and I told them I would play any small part in the film except a blind guy. They told me to select my own part from the movie script, and I discovered the story called for a brief scene with a limo driver. Knowing that it would not and could not involve a blind character, I committed to play the part.

I've repeated that role in four movies, and it's become a tongue-in-cheek oddity or point of interest with movie fans around the world. As a blind guy driving a limo in a movie, I had to figure out how to master all of the elements in operating a motor vehicle. When I asked friends or colleagues to describe the process, they invariably oversimplified it by saying, "You just turn the ignition key, back out of the garage, and drive away."

While I was not in the habit of driving a car, I knew there was a lot more to it than that. When I reminded them, you have to open the door, get in, close the door, put on your seatbelt, and begin the entire process of driving, it became apparent that everyone who has operated a car for any length of time has reduced the entire process to a mindless habit.

Drivers' education students trying to qualify for their license are generally unsteady and quite halting in their driving because they have to think through each step. But after a few short months, they can drive through dense traffic a few feet from other motorists and never even think about all the functions they are performing.

You and I can succeed in our lives and in our finances by driving the process as a routine habit.

<hr />

Many years ago, I read a little book that described how to become an automatic millionaire. At that time in my life, I had no idea how to become a millionaire or even how to get out of debt. Still, I was very interested in doing it, so I thought if there were an automatic way to become a millionaire, I wanted to learn about it. The book was not terribly informative regarding where to invest your money, but it explained a technique regarding how to invest your money that changed my life.

Succeeding in your finances, or in any other area of your life, is a matter of making a series of good decisions. By investing automatically and having the funds removed from your account each month, you take the risk of making bad decisions out of the equation.

Recently, in one of these Winners' Wisdom columns entitled *Today and Tomorrow*, I wrote about university students at the Stovall Center for Entrepreneurship asking me how they should invest the thousands of dollars they won in our annual Launch Competition in which students design, develop, and begin their own businesses.

As I told the students and wrote in the column, I recommended they spend 30% of the funds on current business operations, 60% on cash reserves and future growth, and the remaining 10% they should enjoy as a reward for their success in this milestone achievement. Several readers of that week's column from around the world contacted

> Succeeding in your finances, or in any other area of your life, is a matter of making a series of good decisions.

me, pointing out that I had not recommended the students give away any of their money. As I explained to those readers then and will explain to you now, the students at the Stovall Center for Entrepreneurship have all been taught that giving, taxes, and long-term investing should automatically come off the top of every dollar they earn.

By simply making good decisions one time and arranging your banking appropriately, you will always be a generous giver, avoid tax problems, and systematically invest in your future as an automatic millionaire.

As you go through your day today, take the guesswork out of it, and put your success on autopilot.

Today's the day!

The most efficient, quickest, and easiest way to accomplish anything is to make the tasks involved a regular habit.

41

Contempt and Apathy

Shortly after losing my eyesight, I became frustrated with my inability to enjoy movies and television as I had done throughout my life up to that time. I believe opportunities come disguised as problems. I often remind the university students at the Stovall Center for Entrepreneurship that all you have to do to have a great idea is go through your daily routine, wait for something bad to happen, and ask yourself, "How could I have avoided that?"

Furthermore, the only thing you have to do to turn your great idea into a great business is to ask one more question, "How can I help other people avoid that?" The world will give you fame and fortune as well as contentment if you will just care about others and solve their problems. My late, great friend and mentor Zig Ziglar often said, "You can have everything out of life you want, if you help enough other people get what they want."

I launched the Narrative Television Network, which makes movies and television accessible for 13 million blind and visually impaired Americans and countless others around the world. In the late 1990s the President's Committee on Equal Opportunity named me as Entrepreneur of the Year. The publicity surrounding that recognition caught the attention of Steve Forbes

> "You can have everything out of life you want, if you help enough other people get what they want."

who featured me and the Narrative Television Network in a book released in the spring of 2000 titled, *Forbes Great Success Stories: Twelve Tales of Victory Wrested from Defeat.* I was privileged to be highlighted along with 11 other world class entrepreneurs. But the best thing that came out of that project was my lifelong friendship with Steve Forbes.

I actually featured him doing a cameo playing himself in the movie based on my book titled *The Lamp,* which starred Academy Award-winner Louis Gossett Jr. To promote the release of that film, I did an extended interview with Steve Forbes in his late father's library in the Forbes building.

For years, Mr. Forbes and I have gotten together whenever my travels take me to New York, and we carve out time to sit in that special library and discuss success, money, public policy, and a myriad of topics. I was proud to share one of those conversations through the promotional video for *The Lamp* movie. If you would like to see that video, just contact me at jim@jimstovall.com.

Mr. Forbes is in the minority of multimillionaires as he inherited his wealth. While he has had great success in growing the Forbes' business and his personal wealth, he really never experienced poverty or financial struggles. But he has done a wonderful job staying emotionally connected to the real needs of everyday people.

As you and I build, manage, and enjoy our wealth, we need to be mindful of others and grateful for what we have. That which we exercise, we grow and improve. That which we ignore, we rapidly lose.

You have no doubt heard it said that familiarity breeds contempt. In much the same way, I believe abundance breeds apathy. Recently, here in North America, there was a solar eclipse that was visible to a large segment of the population. Many people took time off work or school and traveled great distances to observe this celestial phenomenon for a few brief moments.

While I certainly understand and applaud people's desire and efforts to experience the eclipse, I wonder what would happen if we lived in a world where a sunset could only be viewed once a decade. We would look on this nightly miraculous lightshow in a much different way. As a blind person myself, one of the sights I miss is the sunset. As my eyesight faded I wrote a song, titled

Sunset, that sealed that visual experience in my mind. I played my *Sunset* song on one of singer/songwriter, Kelly Morrison's albums, and if you would like to hear it, here is the link: https://soundcloud.com/kellymorrison/sunset.

What if we lived in a world in which we could only read ten books throughout our entire life? We would certainly scrutinize the titles we selected and savor the process of reading each of them.

What if we lived in a world where we could only express our love, devotion, or respect to family and friends once a month? We would no doubt plan and emphasize every encounter.

Thankfully, we don't live in those worlds, but contempt due to familiarity and apathy resulting from abundance can skew our perspective. Fortunately, there are antidotes for both conditions. Apathy can be cured with gratitude, and mindfulness can overcome contempt.

Those who have heard me speak, read my books, watched the movies based upon them, or consumed these weekly columns are familiar with the Golden List. The Golden List is a lifelong habit I received as a legacy from my grandmother. It is simply the process of daily listing ten things for which we are thankful. The mere act of regular gratitude eliminates apathy just as light removes shadows and darkness.

Familiarity can be combatted and eliminated with habitual mindfulness. Have you ever routinely done something that became so familiar that you no longer think about it? As part of my morning routine, I peel and eat an orange. It became such a habit that it slipped into my subconscious, and I wasn't really aware I was doing it until my father told me about his childhood in the depths of the Great Depression.

During those difficult times, he had high hopes and eager anticipation that he might receive a single orange in his Christmas stocking that hung on the fireplace mantle. Obviously, getting a fresh tropical fruit in the middle of winter during the depression was an occasion to relish. Since I came to understand the magic and the miracle of this citrus fruit, I am focused and mindful each day as I peel and eat my orange.

I have long believed that we change our lives when we change our minds. As you create a better world for yourself in the future, don't forget to be grateful for the world you live in now as you mindfully experience every bit of it.

As you go through your day today, don't forget your daily vitamins of mindfulness and gratitude.

Today's the day!

42

The Center of Democracy

I wrote the following column more than a decade ago, but every element of it rings as true now as it did then. It is impossible to discuss building wealth or living a millionaire lifestyle without confronting public policy. Excluding philanthropic gifts from my foundation, the 10 largest checks I've ever written, including paying cash for my home, were for taxes. As you build and manage wealth, you want to maximize every expenditure and taxes will be among the largest costs you will pay.

When you become a millionaire, you are in the minority; and when you live in a democracy or representative republic where the majority rules, the government of, by, and for the people will be made up of families struggling with money and financial concerns. The easy and simple battle cry is, "Tax the rich." This begs the question, who are the rich?

Ironically, I've discovered that most people define others who are wealthy or rich as those who have more money than they have themselves. Our free enterprise system has given me everything

I have, and I'm certainly proud and pleased to pay my fair share of taxes. But like any other price I pay, I want to make sure the expenditure is wise and impactful.

As you become a millionaire, you will not only discover that you will have more discretionary income, but you also have more time. You should invest part of this time and money in the political process and get involved.

⬥

This past summer during a trip to Washington, DC, I accepted an invitation to have lunch at the White House. Someone mentioned to me in passing that the White House, and more particularly the Oval Office, was the "Center of Democracy." While I certainly understand the logic behind the statement, somehow it didn't totally ring true in my own perception.

After some thought and pondering it dawned on me that if I had to label a place as the "Center of Democracy," it would be the voting booth. As the presidential election approaches here in the United States, I fear that too many Americans may have overlooked the power of the polling place and the sacred privilege of voting.

Among civilized democratic countries, America ranks extremely low in voter participation. While Belgium, Turkey, Sweden, South Korea, Denmark, and Iceland all have between 80 and 90 percent of their citizens regularly turning out to vote, barely half of Americans bother to cast a ballot. I realize that the combative and confrontational nature of the current campaign causes many people to lose interest and even respect for the process. It is important to remember that democracy works because it is based upon "We the People."

I've heard many people express the notion that they were disgusted with all the candidates and the campaign in general; therefore, they are not planning to vote at all. Even if you are forced to cast your ballot for the least objectionable candidate, I believe it is critical that we all participate in the process.

While there are many great democratic countries around the world, I'm convinced that America is still the last best hope for people everywhere who yearn to be free. Our country was based on the notion that there should not be taxation without rep-

> If I had to label a place as the "Center of Democracy," it would be the voting booth.

resentation. When people today don't bother to vote for their representation, they lose the right to complain about taxation or any other function of government. We are a government of the people, by the people, and for the people, but when people don't participate, the ideals of our way of life begin to fade away.

Dedicated and brave people from Valley Forge, Omaha Beach, and to the current hot spots in the Middle East have risked and sacrificed everything so that you and I could express our free will within the voting booth. When they did so much, how can we do anything less than vote?

As you go through your day today, make plans, preparations, and a commitment to vote.

Today's the day!

43

Financial Offense and Defense

When the following column came out in the summer of 2023, I was shocked to observe the groundswell of interest in the column as well as the two radio shows I do each week based on *Winners' Wisdom*. People seemingly could not wait to see if they had any lost money on account somewhere. One woman told me it's like finding free cash.

While I certainly think it's worth the few moments it will take to see if there are some funds out there in your name, I find it ironic that most people are wasting far more money on a regular basis than they would have ever lost or left behind somewhere. When I meet with families who are trying to get out of debt, I tell them the irrefutable truth that to change their financial condition, they need to earn more, spend less, or, ideally, do both at the same time.

You probably have friends or relatives who periodically ask you to loan them money. They invariably have sad stories about sick children, broken down cars, or other family disasters. While we all would feel inclined to help someone with an illness in their family, when you give most people cash, you are actually funding the most ridiculous expenditures they made during the previous months. If instead of telling you about their sick child, they gave you the true picture—which invariably involves losing money at the casino, overindulgent parties with friends, or buying clothes they didn't need at the mall—you would be less motivated to help solve their problems.

The next time you help someone with a family financial disaster, let them know that your money comes with strings attached, which involves them committing to having an emergency fund so their next crisis will be resolved before it happens.

Becoming a millionaire should not be mystifying or mysterious. It is simply a matter of making every dollar work for you as hard as you worked for it.

<hr />

Recently, I ran across a resource where people can check to see if they are owed any refunds by the U.S. government or corporate entities. If you would like to see if there's money out there waiting for you, visit: https://www.missingmoney.com.

I have shared this resource with a number of family and friends to check it out, and they collectively have already found several thousand dollars. As Benjamin Franklin is known for saying, "A penny saved is a penny earned." This expression has never been more true than in the financial environment we find ourselves in today.

A recent survey showed that as many as 40% of working Americans have a second job or side hustle where they earn extra money through their own small businesses. This research showed that the average individual earns approximately $800 each month from their moonlighting, with many people earning as little as $200-$300 per month working evenings or weekends. To get a true picture of what people are really earning, they must deduct taxes and the costs of commuting, parking, childcare, and other expenses associated with the second income.

While I applaud anyone willing to do extra work to get out of debt, get ahead, or save for future expenses, we must remember that the quickest way to fill up our financial tank is to make sure it's not leaking. If someone is working because they enjoy their second career or they are working to build their side hustle into a full-time business that will become their career, this is wonderful.

However, if someone is giving up evenings or weekends with their family and friends to earn a few hundred dollars—simply trading their time for someone else's money—they need to first be sure that they don't have several hundred dollars already leaking from their financial tank. We all need to periodically look at our

> Don't trade your time for useless stuff that doesn't matter.

checking accounts, our credit card statements, and all of our expenditures to ensure that all of our money is being efficiently utilized in the pursuit of our goals.

If you are trading your free time for a modest amount of money in a dead-end second job, you are giving up your valuable time. The solution to your perceived current financial crisis may be as simple as canceling subscriptions you're not using, getting rid of memberships you don't want, or wasting your hard-earned money on things that don't matter.

You can always earn, save, or invest more money, but you can't replace your time. Don't trade it for useless stuff that doesn't matter.

As you go through your day today, evaluate your earnings, save all you can, and enjoy the fruits of your labor.

Today's the day!

44

The Equation

For most of my adult life, through my books, movies, speeches, radio shows, and weekly *Winners' Wisdom* columns, I have been involved in the personal development, self-help, and success field. There are countless people spending unimaginable amounts of time and money looking for magic pills or secrets that do not exist. The good news is your path to becoming a millionaire is deceptively simple, but it is never easy. The bad news is that there are no secrets and the only path involves hard work, diligence, and discipline.

During my college years as I was losing my sight, I was fortunate enough to meet an elderly gentleman who became one of my mentors in matters relating to finances and entrepreneurship. When I asked this octogenarian, self-made millionaire how I could become a wealthy entrepreneur, he told me, "Always do what you say you're going to do, deliver more than you promise, and create value in the lives of other people."

> "Always do what you say you're going to do, deliver more than you promise, and create value in the lives of other people."

As an immature college student, I was underwhelmed and disappointed with his answer as I remained convinced that there was some kind of magic spell that millionaires knew that the rest of us didn't know. Now, almost 50 years later, I've discovered that my mentor's underlying truths are real, powerful, and have made me a millionaire entrepreneur. It's much like Dorothy's friends in *The Wizard of Oz*. They went through a difficult ordeal on a quest to find courage, knowledge, and love. When they finally confronted the wizard, he showed them that they already possessed everything they were seeking.

I offer my contact information in each of my over 50 books and more than a thousand weekly Winners' Wisdom columns—including the one you're reading right now. With millions of books in print and countless people around the world reading this column each week in newspapers, magazines, and online publications, you can imagine that we have a lot of people who reach out to us.

Besides people's kind and encouraging comments about my writing, which I always appreciate, the most common topics people ask about are financial independence, physical fitness, and having great personal relationships. In these three areas, as in most things in life, we all have more than enough information and knowledge to be successful already. We don't fail because we don't know what to do; we fail because we don't do what we know.

Within each of these three vital areas of our lives, there are simple principles and equations that can bring us success. Please note I said "simple," not "easy." It's very simple to tell someone how to complete a marathon. You just run a little over 26 miles until you get to the finish line. It's incredibly simple, but anyone who has completed a marathon will assure you it's not easy.

To be financially independent, you must spend less than you earn and put the excess funds to work for you. All wealth is built using this simple equation. It's not complicated, but it's never easy. To become physically fit, you must burn more calories than you eat while building muscle. Virtually all of us have known how to do this for years, but we've put very little time, effort, and energy into doing it.

Having a great relationship involves being willing to give more than you receive. It is a matter of being committed to reaching out more than halfway to connect with your significant other. While most people think it's a matter of finding the right person, reality tells us it's a matter of being the right person.

My late, great friend and colleague Brian Klemmer wrote a book entitled *If How-To's Were Enough, We Would All Be Skinny,*

Rich & Happy. It was a gift to be able to work with Brian during his life; and today, I am privileged to be able to continue building upon his legacy through my work with Klemmer & Associates. As Brian's book title implies, if you want to change your life, you need to look beyond the current fads and magic pills, go back to the time-tested equations you already know, and revisit them with a new attitude, commitment, and mindset.

As you go through your day today, focus on doing more with what you already know.

Today's the day!

45

Success and Service

I t's difficult for me to admit to my readers and those who hear my speeches in arena events and business conventions that, for over half of my adult life, I labored under a false assumption or only a partial truth regarding how to build wealth and success. As a young man mired in debt and struggling to adjust to the world as a blind person, I was hopeless and helpless. At that time, I believed success was simply a matter of going from poverty to prosperity.

Now, I often say and repeatedly write that success involves going from poverty to prosperity, but then requires you to move into purpose. When you first begin your journey, getting out of debt and acquiring some things you've always wanted will be enough to keep you motivated. But eventually, just acquiring more stuff becomes a hollow existence that won't inspire you to get out of bed in the morning.

At this writing, I've continued to work for more than 20 years beyond the point when I had more than enough money to live

> Success involves going from poverty to prosperity, but then requires you to move into purpose.

comfortably for the rest of my life. I remain motivated and productive because there are people and causes that continue to matter to me. I consider my friend and colleague Don Green, who runs the Napoleon Hill Foundation, to be one of the premiere thought leaders in the 21st century. He is committed to keeping Napoleon Hill's timeless principles relevant by combining them with up-to-the-minute practical advice. Don and I co-authored a book titled *The Gift of Giving,* which deals with the world beyond your own wants and needs.

My foundation has provided college scholarships for more than 500 students over the past couple of decades. Every year, our scholarship committee goes through all of the applications and ranks them from best to worst. Starting with the most qualified, we begin going through each of the applications and assign an amount of money we will award them to pay for their education.

Invariably, we run out of funds before we run out of applications. Every year, I am inspired and recommitted by the first application that emerges beyond the point when we have exhausted our funds. That young person's story, along with their hopes and dreams, keeps me motivated for one more year.

Paying off debt and acquiring a supply of stuff in your life can be accomplished fairly quickly, but helping others and changing the world will give you more than enough to do in many lifetimes.

⁕ ——— ⁕ ——— ⁕

Recently, I've had two new books released, so I've been doing a lot of interviews to promote the titles. Thankfully, one of the books immediately jumped onto the bestseller list, and I had an interviewer ask me, "Do you write books to help other people or just to create financial success for yourself?"

The answer is quite simply, "Yes." I cannot separate serving others from financial success. I have said for years that people who have a goal to make money don't understand how the system works. The only people who really make money work at the mint and create currency. The rest of us must earn money, and this is accomplished by creating value in the lives of other people.

If you want to create wealth, your goals should not involve your own financial situation, but instead, they should involve helping more people in increasingly significant ways. Money is among the most misunderstood commodities in the world. It is a result, not a cause. Too many people feel they should be guaranteed money before they create any value. This is like the poor, misguided soul who stands in front of a cold fireplace and declares, "Give me some heat and then I will throw in some wood."

If you're going to understand money, you have to understand the terms surrounding it. Wealth is simply the resources required for you and your family to have the things in your life you want. In addition to the things you want, you should have a cash reserve and a plan for giving to organizations and causes that matter to you. Once you've touched all these bases, you have achieved wealth on your own terms regardless of how much money is required.

Financial independence is being able to live off the return of your accumulated wealth. Once your investments generate enough money for you to live, you are financially independent, and it is no longer necessary for you to trade your time for someone else's money. This does not mean you won't work in some capacity that matters to you. Most financially independent people I know continue to work. However, they no longer do things that don't matter to them simply to earn money.

Once you understand the terms and grasp the relationship between success and service, you can progress down the path that leads to your goals. You will need to continue to monitor your progress and your motivations as building wealth, financial independence, and personal success requires constant course corrections much like piloting a jet on a flight to the destination of your goals and dreams.

As you go through your day today, make your money work for you as hard as you work for it.

Today's the day!

46

The Price of Tuition

Here in the 21st century, it's virtually impossible to have a strategy involving becoming a millionaire or creating wealth without dealing with college tuition and student loan debt. I'm a huge believer in higher education. One of the first philanthropic projects I launched after creating my own wealth involved the Crusader Scholarship Fund. This fund has provided scholarships for more than 500 students in the past 30 years, so it's easy to see that I believe in the process.

However, it's important to explore both cost and value. Far too many young people and their families believe that student loan debt is the only way to get a college degree. They really don't carefully compare and evaluate the cost of tuition at various institutions because it's really not coming out of their pocket; it's simply a nebulous balance that they will have to pay at some undetermined point in the future.

Student loan debt is real, and it can derail millionaire aspirations for students, parents, and even grandparents. When you understand the value of money or the cost of debt over a long period of time, you come face to face with the reality that student loans can destroy your financial strategies at the most critical point in time.

I work with many college students through my scholarships and the Stovall Center for Entrepreneurship, which offers degrees to students from around the world. Even with the high cost of tuition, I have seen students take advantage of community colleges for their first two years, and then combine work-study, private scholarships, and grants to get a four-year degree and even go to graduate school without creating debt.

As we have discussed in this book, before you can become a millionaire, you have to get out of the hole you have created by your debt. Student loans are a big contributor to this problem.

◆———————◆———————◆

While founding and being involved with the Stovall Center for Entrepreneurship at Oral Roberts University, I have the privilege of working with college students from over a hundred nations who are getting their degrees and learning how to run their own businesses. If you follow the headlines, you are undoubtedly aware that college tuition is extremely high and continues to rise with no end in sight. One fascinating element of college tuition is that you pay the price whether or not you learn the lesson and apply it to your life.

Our experiences in the real world are another form of tuition. Opportunities come to us disguised as problems, and each crisis offers us a lesson for our personal and professional lives, whether or not we learn the lesson. Success, to a great extent, involves taking the information or the lessons we have been given and applying them in our lives.

> **Before you can become a millionaire, you have to get out of the hole you have created by your debt.**

Knowledge is simply being aware of the information. Wisdom consists of putting the information into practice and making it work for us. Failure is the tuition we pay for the lessons never learned. I'm often reminded of the great lyrics Billy Joel wrote in his song *The Entertainer.* "I am the entertainer, and I've had to pay my price. The things I did not know at first, I learned by doin' twice."

Winston Churchill said, "Those who do not learn from history are destined to repeat it." While this is undoubtedly valid from a global or historical perspective, it is equally true in our personal or professional lives. We all make mistakes from time to time and find ourselves in a proverbial hole. The quickest way to get out of the hole is to stop digging. Smart people learn from their mistakes, and the wisest among us learn from other people's mistakes. They don't have to burn themselves on the hot stove if they just saw someone else do it.

Whether you're raising your children, teaching students, or trying to succeed in your own life, never allow a mistake to be made without a corresponding change. Failure is fertilizer if we learn from it and apply it to our future. Otherwise, it just smells bad and will continue to reproduce more and greater failure in the future.

As you go through your day today, learn from failure and embrace success.

Today's the day!

47

Investing 101

Of my more than 50 books, approximately half of them are novels, nine of which have been turned into movies thus far. While I certainly intend for all of my plots in these movies and novels to be entertaining, I always want there to be valuable life lessons. One of my movie partners, who was the founder of a large financial planning organization in Boston, often said, "If you can tell a great story, you earn the right to share your message."

In my novel entitled *One Season of Hope*, I highlight a young high school football player battling cancer and trying to play football in his senior season. During that story, there's a point where the school officials are meeting to discuss a multimillion-dollar renovation of the stadium. As everyone was forecasting gloom and doom as they described why it would never be possible to pay for the project, one of the school teachers calmly announced she would just donate the money herself. Not only did it make a great storyline, but it's based on a true story.

People around the world with relatively modest incomes and elementary investing strategies have become multimillionaires. I recount one such story in the following column. This story is very special to me because it was my father.

———◆———

Sometimes, we get so deep into the details of a topic that we forget to focus on the basics. This time of year, people throughout North America and around the world are caught up in the frenzy of college or professional football. There are 24-hour-a-day radio stations and media outlets that constantly focus on the most subtle nuances of every play in every game. While there may be some merit to this, football always has and always will come down to the basics of blocking and tackling. The team that can manage the basics by blocking and tackling well will inevitably win the game, regardless of the sophistication and exotic design the other team may employ.

When it comes to investing, it's imperative that we get back to the basics. In my youth, I went to countless free investment seminars put on by banks, insurance companies, and brokerage firms. These seminars were thinly veiled sales pitches to lure new clients. They all seemed to begin the same way. The speaker for the evening would render his credentials as a financial expert and then verbalize the following assumption, "Let's say you have $100,000 available today to invest." I sat there thinking I didn't have a hundred dollars to invest, and I doubted if any of my fellow audience members had much more than I did. At this writing, over 80% of Americans have less than $100,000, even including their retirement funds. So, let's begin at the beginning.

The first rule of successful investing is spending less than you earn. This rule is not as simple as it sounds, as our elected officials have not mastered this concept. Only when you have money left over at the end of the month can you begin to consider investing. Unfortunately, the majority of people have month left over at the end of the money. If you find yourself in this position, which I had in my youth, your only options are to earn more, spend less, or both.

> Spend less than you earn. Only when you have money left over at the end of the month can you begin to consider investing.

Once you have some discretionary money to invest at the end of the month, and before you consider stocks, bonds, real estate, gold, or any other investment, you should eliminate all of your consumer debt. This elimination includes credit cards, personal loans, car loans, student loans, and any other obligation you may have other than your home mortgage. If it's going to take more than a few years to pay off these debts, you will want to participate in funding your retirement while you're eliminating your debt, particularly if your employer offers matching contributions.

Once you have touched all of these bases, you can join the shockingly small number of people who are at the starting line of the investment race. There are no good or bad investments. You should select your vehicle based on your temperament, talent, and expertise in any given field.

I just recently helped settle an estate for a gentleman who never earned close to a six-figure income, never invested in equities of any kind, and only put his money in government-guaranteed investments. While most self-proclaimed financial experts would tell you this is a recipe for failure, this gentleman started with nothing and accumulated several million dollars throughout his lifetime. You can do well in the investment race with a variety of vehicles if you take care of all the details before you line up to begin the investment race.

As you go through your day today, focus on the basics, and the details will take care of themselves.

Today's the day!

48

Next Step

In the following column, I cite two giants in the field of success and two of the greatest mentors in my life. Without Dr. Waitley and Dr. Schuller, I would have never written my first book much less more than 50. When I think of these amazing gentlemen, I think of the two principles that will be critical to your financial success. One is *get started today.* If you have a 30-year financial plan culminating in your retirement, the thirtieth year will be worth hundreds of thousands of dollars to you. That valuable year doesn't begin decades from now. It begins today because if you don't get started, your 30-year plan will only be 29 years or may never get started at all.

Dr. Waitley also taught me the difference between wealth and treasures. As you and I are striving to build wealth and become millionaires, we don't want to lose sight of the treasures in our lives. Years ago, there was a devastating fire at Dr. Waitley's home. Since he was an author and speaker, he worked from home so the fire totally destroyed his house, his business, and his automobiles. As he ran from the house and rushed toward the mailbox at the street, which was the designated meeting place where he and his family had determined to gather in case of a crisis, he was grateful to see his wife, all their children, and even the family pets safe and sound. When a fireman sadly told Dr. Waitley everything was gone and it was a total loss, he responded, "Everything that matters is right here."

⸺ ◆ ⸺

The journey of a thousand miles does, indeed, begin with the first step, and the journey to your destiny begins with your next step. I have millions of books in print among my over 50 titles, and every book has my contact information in it, so you can imagine how many people I have reaching out to connect with me as I welcome you to do using the contact information below.

Probably the most often-asked question from people who have contacted me over the last 25 years is, "How do I get started?" Many people have a general goal or vague idea of where they would like to be in their life, but it remains somewhere off in the distant future.

My mentor and friend, Denis Waitley, is fond of describing a place he calls "Someday Isle." Someday Isle is a beautiful tropical island where there is no past and no future. Nothing has ever been done there, and nothing ever will be done there because people around the world constantly invoke the name of Someday Isle as they declare, "Someday, I'll..." If you or I have a dream, a goal, or an objective in our lives, it was put there for a reason, and there is something we are supposed to do today that will bring us closer to our destiny. I am saddened as I meet people who have had goals for many years or even decades that they've never really embraced as a reality and taken that first critical step.

Any goal worthy of your time, effort, and energy will invariably be beyond your current capacity. You may not know how to do it, where to do it, when to do it, who to do it with, or where to get the money, but it doesn't mean that you can't start today. Knowledge is power. If you can begin by educating yourself on all elements of reaching your goal and begin connecting with people who have achieved what you want to achieve you will be well on your way.

My late, great colleague and mentor, Dr. Robert Schuller, was fond of saying, "Starting is halfway there." Dr. Schuller was intelligent enough to realize that if you have a goal to go around the world, the act of simply starting doesn't literally transport you halfway around the globe. What he meant was, if you establish an objective and simply begin right where you are, you are way ahead of most people who will never begin at all. Failure rarely occurs at the finish line. Failure happens in the starting blocks.

If you think of your most grandiose and awesome dreams and goals and simply begin moving toward them, they will become a part of your reality and your future.

As you go through your day today, don't let the sun go down before you have taken that first step.

Today's the day!

> "Starting is halfway there."

49

Help or Harm

As you are traveling your lifelong millionaire journey and creating wealth, it's critical to remember that a portion of every dollar should be spent on your immediate needs, a portion should be saved and invested for your future, and a portion should be given away. Remember, giving should involve both your time and your money.

Early in your journey, you may give away more of your time as you are investing your money. Later, you will be able to give away large amounts of money but may have less time. You will need to be as strategic about your giving as you are about your spending budget and your investment strategy.

People who have lived their lives in debt and have no expendable income, have an antidote to friends, family, and organizations seeking money. It's very easy to simply respond, "I don't have any money to give you." Once you become a millionaire, you have to decide where your philanthropic dollars can be best invested. The following column was written to help people start making these fundamental decisions about their giving.

When I was a young boy, my grandfather told me about a man who had been climbing in the mountains and came upon an eagle's nest. He happened to discover it just as the eggs were hatching and the tiny eaglets were struggling their way into the world. This well-intentioned man broke open the eggs freeing the tiny eagles. While he was trying to help them, he unknowingly destroyed them because the struggle of getting out of the egg is what gives a young eagle the strength it will need to survive.

Anyone who attains a minimal level of success or even a degree of enlightenment understands that there is no true and lasting achievement without helping others and making a difference in the world around you. While most everyone would agree on the fact that they want to help others, the act of helping another person is not as easy to identify as you might think.

Abraham Lincoln said, "The worst thing you can do for anyone you care about is anything that they can do on their own." People who are given things, opportunities, and solutions without earning or paying for them often are harmed more than they are helped. Wealth without work, position without effort, and remedy without resource is seldom positive in the long run. The majority of lottery winners are in worse financial condition five years after their winning number is called than they were before playing the lottery. They suffer a much higher divorce rate and instance of drug abuse and alcoholism.

> "The worst thing you can do for anyone you care about is anything that they can do on their own."

At some point in life, all mature people learn that actions have consequences—either good or bad. The sooner we can learn this lesson, the more productive and peaceful life we will have. If you shelter a child from all consequences of their decisions, you may protect them temporarily from a few bumps or scrapes. Unfortunately, you may relegate them to making a poor decision during a life-or-death situation. We all need to learn that the stove is hot—one time—the hard way. From then on, we are cautious around stoves and begin to consider the consequences of other decisions.

Any study of successful people in our society will reveal a disproportionate number of underprivileged immigrants achieving great success in a relatively short period of time. There is nothing innate about financial struggles, language barriers, and cultural challenges that make people succeed. It is simply that enduring problems and overcoming barriers is a habit that, once learned, carries over into every area of our lives.

That person that turned you down for help may have done you the greatest favor of all. Self-reliance and independence are critical parts of succeeding in life. All of us have received a hand up at one time or another, and hopefully have offered the same to those coming along behind us; but it is important to be sure that we are helping and not harming those we care about.

As you go through your day today, look for ways to assist others, and eliminate any harm you're doing by trying to help in ways people can perform on their own.

Today's the day!

50

Think and Do It Now

In this last chapter of this book, it is my fervent hope that our journey together toward your financial independence is not ending but instead is just starting. In the coming days you will need to start building your own dream team including a lawyer, a CPA, and an investment professional. They will help you with the specific steps you will need to take based on your situation.

While I'm always available to provide financial advice to the readers of my books and columns around the world, generic financial advice can be as dangerous as a generic medical diagnosis. I am a licensed financial professional, and I have written several books dealing specifically with building wealth. I have gone from poverty and debt to financial independence and have become a multimillionaire. But I continue to work with my own dream team.

The chapters in this book come directly from my *Winners' Wisdom* column, which is read by people around the world. If you would like to receive my weekly column, take my Millionaire Map Assessment or Productivity Profile free of charge, or ask your own financial questions and share your millionaire milestones with me, I am always available via jim@jimstovall.com.

If you don't get started immediately after finishing this book, it is likely you will never become a millionaire because it is likely you will never get started. As you will see in the following column, people either never form a basic plan and fall victim to randomness, or they procrastinate waiting for a better time that simply never comes.

When I was where you likely are and contemplating my own struggle to eliminate debt and become a millionaire, I imagined what it might be like. I can assure you the millionaire lifestyle is better than I ever imagined.

Regular readers of this weekly *Winners' Wisdom* column in newspapers, magazines, and online publications around the world know that my father passed away recently. While it's sad and difficult, it is gratifying to look back on his 92-year life and know he was happy, healthy, and productive right up to the end. The ensuing months have given me an opportunity to revisit and enjoy many fond memories of him and the profound lessons he taught me.

During my grade school years, my father was the chief executive officer of an organization and in charge of leading and

> If you don't get started immediately after finishing this book, it is likely you will never become a millionaire....

managing over 400 employees. He was a great list-maker and constantly wrote things down that he needed to check on or follow up with. He encouraged all his employees to make lists. He often said, "If it's worth doing, it's worth writing down. You don't even go to the grocery store without a list to keep you from forgetting something."

He gave out hundreds of pocket-sized notebooks for his staff to keep their lists of priorities and tasks. I will never forget that these pocket-sized notebooks all had one of two inscriptions on the cover. Some of the notebooks simply said, "Think," while others said, "Do it now."

I assumed he handed them out randomly, but when I asked him about it, he explained that there are two kinds of people. There are those who don't think before they act. They are prone to knee-jerk reactions that create a lot of errors that must be cleaned up or repaired. These people need to think about each activity and its consequences and alternatives before acting.

The second group of people received my father's notebook with the inscription on the cover, "Do it now." These people, as he explained to me, are procrastinators and over-analyzers. They are waiting for all the lights to turn green before they leave the house or for conditions to be perfect. Conditions are never perfect, and we are often called upon to make decisions and act before we have all the information we would like.

My father divided his employees into those who needed to think more before they acted and those who needed to act before they overanalyzed. There's a little bit of both groups in each of us. If we are to succeed in our personal and professional lives, we must strike a balance between black and white and live in the gray world of consistent compromise.

As you go through your day today, consider everything, but don't fail to act.

Today's the day!

About
Jim Stovall

In spite of blindness, Jim Stovall has been a National Olympic weightlifting champion, a successful investment broker, the President of the Emmy Award-winning Narrative Television Network, and a highly sought-after author and platform speaker.

He is the author of more than 50 books, including the best-seller, *The Ultimate Gift,* which is now a major motion picture from 20th Century Fox starring James Garner and Abigail Breslin. Eight of his other novels have also been made into movies with two more in production.

Steve Forbes, president and CEO of *Forbes* magazine, says, "Jim Stovall is one of the most extraordinary men of our era."

For his work in making television accessible to our nation's 13 million blind and visually impaired people, The President's Committee on Equal Opportunity selected Jim Stovall as the Entrepreneur of the Year.

Jim Stovall has been featured in *The Wall Street Journal, Forbes* magazine, *USA Today*, and has been seen on *Good Morning America, CNN,* and *CBS Evening News.* He was also chosen as the International Humanitarian of the Year, joining Jimmy Carter, Nancy Reagan, and Mother Teresa as recipients of this honor.

THANK YOU FOR READING THIS BOOK!

If you found any of the information helpful, please take a few minutes and leave a review on the bookselling platform of your choice.

BONUS GIFT!

Don't forget to sign up to try our newsletter and grab your free personal development ebook here:

soundwisdom.com/classics